CW01572772

EXPLANATORY NOTES

Disability Discrimination Act 2005

Chapter 13

£6.50

DISABILITY DISCRIMINATION ACT

EXPLANATORY NOTES

INTRODUCTION

1.   These explanatory notes relate to the Disability Discrimination Act which received Royal Assent on 7 April 2005. They have been prepared by the Department for Work and Pensions, the Department for Transport (in relation to sections 5 to 9) and the Department for Education and Skills (in relation to section 15) in order to assist the reader of the Act and to help inform debate on it. They do not form part of the Act and have not been endorsed by Parliament.

2.   These notes need to be read in conjunction with the Act. They are not, and are not meant to be, a comprehensive description of the Act. Where a section or part of a section does not seem to require any explanation or comment, none is given.

SUMMARY AND BACKGROUND

3.   The Disability Discrimination Act 2005 ("the 2005 Act") makes substantial amendments to the Disability Discrimination Act 1995 ("the DDA") building on amendments already made to that Act by other legislation since 1999.

4.   The DDA, as originally enacted, contained provisions making it unlawful to discriminate against a disabled person in relation to employment, the provision of goods, facilities and services, and the disposal and management of premises. It also contained some provisions relating to education; and enabled the Secretary of State for Transport to make regulations with a view to facilitating the accessibility of taxis, public service vehicles and rail vehicles for disabled people.

5.   In December 1997, the Government established the Disability Rights Task Force, an independent body comprising members from disability organisations, the private and public sectors and trade unions, to advise it on how best to meet its 1997 manifesto commitment to look at securing comprehensive and enforceable civil rights for disabled people. As a result of the Task Force's first recommendations, the Government established, in April 2000, the Disability Rights Commission. (The constitution and functions of the Commission are set out in the Disability Rights

Commission Act 1999.)

6.   In December 1999, the Task Force published its final report to Government: "From Exclusion to Inclusion". This recommended a number of major extensions to the DDA's coverage and refinements to its detail.

7.   The Government published an interim response to the Task Force's recommendations in 2000 and, in March 2001, published its final response "Towards Inclusion – Civil Rights for Disabled People". That response, which was also a consultation document, set out the Government's proposals for taking forward those of the Task Force's recommendations with which it agreed. One immediate response was to introduce the Special Educational Needs and Disability Act 2001 which extended the DDA so as to make it unlawful to discriminate against disabled pupils and students seeking access to education in schools and colleges.

8.   The Government has already taken forward the main employment proposals set out in "Towards Inclusion" in the Disability Discrimination Act 1995 (Amendment) Regulations 2003[1] ("the Amendment Regulations"), made under section 2(2) of the European Communities Act 1972 in order to implement the disability aspects of the EC Employment Directive (2000/78/EC). These Regulations, which came into force on 1 October 2004, make significant changes to the DDA which were also proposed by the Task Force including: ending the exemption of small employers from the scope of the DDA; and bringing within its ambit a number of excluded occupations, such as the police, fire-fighters, prison officers and partners in business partnerships. The Regulations also make other changes not proposed by the Task Force. (See also the Disability Discrimination (Pensions) Regulations 2003[2], which amend Part 2 DDA to bring its provisions into line with Directive 2000/78/EC in relation to discrimination concerning occupational pension schemes.)

9.   The 2005 Act takes forward the Government's remaining proposals. A draft Bill was published in December 2003 for pre-legislative scrutiny. It was considered by a Joint Committee of both Houses, who reported their findings on 27 May 2004. The Government published its response to the Joint Committee's report on 15 July 2004. Further details can be viewed on the Department for Work and Pensions' disability website (www.disability.gov.uk). The 2005 Act contains provisions giving effect to many of the Committee's recommendations, as well as new provisions which did not appear in the draft Bill: see in particular sections 6 to 8 (rail vehicles), section 9 (disabled persons' parking badges), section 15 (general qualifications bodies) and section 16 (improvements to let dwelling houses).

---

[1] S.I. 2003/1673.
[2] S.I. 2003/2770.

TERRITORIAL EXTENT

10.   The 2005 Act extends to Great Britain, save for section 9 and the related disabled persons' "blue badge" parking provisions and section 16 (improvements to let dwelling houses), both of which extend only to England and Wales. Provision corresponding to the "blue badge" provisions already applies in Scotland, and the Scottish Executive is considering what steps to take in relation to disability-related adaptations to people's homes.

11.   Equal opportunities are in principle reserved to the Westminster Parliament, but the imposition of duties on office-holders in the Scottish administration, on any Scottish public authority with mixed functions or no reserved functions, or on cross-border public authorities in respect of their Scottish functions is an exception to this rule and falls within the devolved competence of the Scottish Parliament[3]. Section 3 of the 2005 Act imposes duties on public authorities with the aim of promoting equality of opportunity for disabled people. This therefore falls partly within the competence of the Scottish Parliament. The Scottish Parliament has confirmed (on 24 February 2005) that it is content for Parliament to legislate for Scotland in this devolved area.

12.   The 2005 Act does not extend to Northern Ireland since disability discrimination and transport are "transferred matters" under the Northern Ireland Act 1998. As regards Wales, the 2005 Act confers no new powers on the National Assembly to make orders or regulations, save in relation to section 9 (the "blue badge" parking provisions).

SUMMARY

13.   The 2005 Act's measures:

Public authorities

i)   **Section 1**: bring councillors, and members of the Greater London Authority, within the scope of the DDA;

ii)   **Section 2**: ensure that, with some exceptions, functions of public authorities not already covered by the DDA are brought within its scope (so that it would be unlawful for a public authority, without justification, to discriminate against a disabled person when exercising its functions);

iii)   **Section 3**: introduce a new duty on public authorities requiring them, when exercising their functions, to have due regard to the need to eliminate harassment of and unlawful discrimination against disabled persons, to promote positive attitudes towards disabled persons, to encourage participation by disabled persons in public

---

[3] See section L2 of Part 2 of Schedule 5 to the Scotland Act 1998.

life, and to promote equality of opportunity between disabled persons and other persons;

iv)   **Section 4**: amend section 64A of the DDA so as to clarify who the correct defendant is in the case of a claim of discrimination being made against a police officer under Part 3 of the DDA and authorise payment of compensation from the police fund in relation to such a claim;

Transport

v)   **Section 5:** provide that the current exemption from section 19 to 21 of the DDA (which deal with the provision of goods, facilities and services to the public) for transport services extends only to transport vehicles themselves, and create a power to enable that exemption to be lifted for different vehicles at different times and to differing extents;

vi)   **Section 6:** amend the definition of 'rail vehicle' in Part 5 of the DDA to enable rail vehicle accessibility regulations to be applied to all rail vehicles, enable the regulations to be applied to the refurbishment of rail vehicles, clarify and extend the current power to grant exemptions from the requirements, change the exemption process and include a requirement for the Secretary of State to produce an annual report on the making of exemptions;

vii)   **Section 7:** introduce new provisions requiring rail vehicle accessibility compliance certificates to be obtained for prescribed rail vehicles;

viii)   **Section 8:** replace the existing criminal offence for use of a rail vehicle which does not conform with rail vehicle accessibility regulations with a civil enforcement system, and set out the procedure for imposing civil penalties, including a right of appeal to a court;

ix)   **Section 9:** amend the Chronically Sick and Disabled Persons Act 1970 so as to provide for the recognition in England and Wales of disabled persons' parking badges issued outside Great Britain;

Other matters

x)   **Section 10:** amend the DDA's new provision on discriminatory advertisements (section 16B, as inserted by the Amendment Regulations) so as to impose liability on a third party who publishes a discriminatory advertisement (for example, a newspaper) as well as the person placing the advertisement;

xi)   **Section 11:** amend the DDA in respect of group insurance arrangements;

xii)   **Section 12:** bring within the scope of Part 3 of the DDA private clubs with 25 or more members;

xiii)   **Section 13**: impose a duty to provide reasonable adjustments on landlords and others who manage rented premises;

xiv)   **Section 14**: confer a power to modify or end the current small dwellings exemption in section 23 and new sections 24B and 24H (as inserted by section 13 of the 2005 Act) of the DDA;

xv)   **Section 15**: make it unlawful for general qualifications bodies to discriminate against disabled persons in relation to the award of prescribed qualifications;

xvi)   **Section 16**: make provision for cases where a tenant seeks consent to make an improvement to a let dwelling house to facilitate the enjoyment of the premises by a disabled occupier (which could include himself), including provision for the Disability Rights Commission to make available a conciliation service, to provide assistance in legal proceedings in any dispute arising on the landlord's withholding of his consent and to issue codes of practice on consent to such improvements;

xvii)   **Section 17:** extend section 56 of the DDA so as to provide a procedure for questions and replies, not only for claims under Part 2 of the DDA but also for claims under Part 3 of the DDA;

xviii)   **Section 18**: amend the definition of disability in respect of people with mental illnesses; deem people with HIV infection, multiple sclerosis, or cancer to be disabled for the purposes of the DDA; and clarify that there is no implied limitation to the scope of the regulation-making power which enables people to be deemed to be disabled;

Supplementary

xix)   **Sections 19 and 20**: deal with minor and consequential amendments and repeals, the short title, extent and commencement;

xx)   **Schedule 1**: make minor and consequential amendments to the DDA and other enactments;

xxi)   **Schedule 2**: provide for the repeal of provisions contained in the DDA and other enactments.

COMMENTARY ON SECTIONS

Section 1: Councillors

14.   Section 1 inserts new sections 15A, 15B and 15C into Part 2 of the DDA, as amended by the Amendment Regulations. The new provisions make it unlawful for the locally-electable authorities listed in new section 15A(1) to discriminate against their members in relation to the carrying-out of official business.

15.   New section 15A(1) sets out the authorities to which the new provisions apply. These include all local authorities in England, Wales and Scotland and the Greater

London Authority.

16.   The duties imposed on locally-electable authorities by the new provisions only apply where a member is carrying out "official business". By virtue of new section 15A(2), a member carries out official business where he does anything in his capacity as: a member of his own authority; a member of any body to which he is appointed by his own authority or a group of authorities that includes his own authority; or a member of any other public body. Whether an authority actually has power to provide training or other facilities (see new section 15B(1)(a)) to its members for their carrying-out of any particular official business will be determined by the legislation from which the authority derives its powers.

17.   New section 15B(1) makes it unlawful for an authority to discriminate against a disabled member: in relation to opportunities which it affords its members to receive training or any other facility it makes available to its members for the carrying-out of official business; or by subjecting the disabled member to any other detriment in relation to the carrying-out of official business. "Discrimination" bears the meaning set out in section 3A of the DDA (as inserted by the Amendment Regulations).

18.   New section 15B(2) makes it unlawful for an authority to subject a disabled member to harassment in relation to the carrying-out of official business. "Harassment" is defined in section 3B of the DDA (as inserted by the Amendment Regulations).

19.   New section 15B(3) provides for a number of matters to be excluded from the scope of the duties imposed by new section 15B(1). These are: election or appointment to an office of an authority (such as a cabinet post); election or appointment to a committee or sub-committee of an authority, or to an office of a committee or sub-committee (such as chairman); and appointments to any other body to which an authority, or a group of bodies including that authority, has the power to appoint or nominate (such as a police authority).

20.   New section 15B(4) and (5) enable the Secretary of State to make regulations relating to the justification for less favourable treatment. New section 15B(4) permits regulations to be made prescribing the circumstances in which treatment is to be taken to be justified or not to be justified. New section 15B(5) allows regulations made under subsection (4) to modify or disapply the justification for less favourable treatment set out in section 3A(3) of the DDA (as inserted by the Amendment Regulations). However, this power cannot be used to justify less favourable treatment which amounts to direct discrimination, which is defined in section 3A(5) of the DDA (as inserted by the Amendment Regulations).

21.   New section 15B(6) imposes a limitation on the justifications that may be provided for in regulations under section 15B(4). The effect is that an authority which fails to comply with a duty to make a reasonable adjustment in relation to a disabled person cannot justify its treatment unless it would have been justified even if it had complied with the duty. See section 3A(6) of the DDA for a similar

provision which applies to the rest of Part 2 of the DDA.

22.   New section 15C sets out the duty of an authority to make reasonable adjustments in relation to its disabled members and broadly follows the pattern of Part 2 of the Act. An authority will be under a duty to make an adjustment where a provision, criterion or practice it applies, or which is applied on its behalf, or a physical feature of premises which it occupies or controls, places a disabled member at a substantial disadvantage in comparison with non-disabled members in relation to the carrying-out of official business. In these circumstances, an authority will be under a duty to take reasonable steps to prevent the provision, criterion, practice or physical feature from having that effect. Section 15C(3) provides that the duty in subsection (2) does not apply if the authority could not reasonably be expected to know that the member has a disability and is likely to be affected in the way mentioned in subsection (1).

23.   New section 15C(4) enables the Secretary of State to make regulations elaborating on the duty to make adjustments.

24.   A victim of unlawful discrimination or harassment contrary to the new provisions would be able to bring enforcement proceedings in an employment tribunal under section 17A[4] of the DDA.

25.   Schedule 1 includes a number of minor and consequential amendments arising out of new sections 15A to 15C (see the commentary below).

Section 2: Discrimination by public authorities

26.   This section inserts new sections 21B to 21E into the DDA and thereby extends its scope to cover almost all the functions of public authorities. This brings the DDA into line with section 19B of the Race Relations Act 1976 ("RRA") (as inserted by the Race Relations (Amendment) Act 2000, section 1).

27.   In general terms, the effect of the insertion of new sections 21B to 21E into the DDA will be to prohibit discrimination, where not already covered elsewhere in the DDA, in the exercise of all public functions other than (in broad terms) those of legislation, prosecution, judicial acts, and state security. This new prohibition of discrimination will therefore cover decisions by Ministers, local authorities, the police and other governmental organisations. The definition of discrimination is more extensive than its equivalent in the RRA as discrimination can include not making a reasonable adjustment to the way the function is carried out. This might mean that a public authority would have to exercise a function in a different way for a disabled person where it would be reasonable to do so (for example, visiting a person at home rather than requiring them to attend a Government building), or to supplement the exercise of a function with an additional act, where it would be reasonable to do so (such as the provision of an interpreter for a deaf person). An

---

[4] The Amendment Regulations renumber section 8 of the DDA as section 17A.

act that would otherwise amount to discrimination can however be justified in certain circumstances under new section 21D(3) to (5).

28.   A victim of unlawful discrimination contrary to the new provisions could bring enforcement proceedings in the county court (or, in Scotland, in the sheriff court) under section 25 of the DDA.

New section 21B: Discrimination by public authorities

29.   New section 21B(1) makes it unlawful for a public authority to discriminate against a disabled person in carrying out its functions. It should be noted, however, that section 21B(1) is subject to section 59 of the DDA. This means that section 21B(1) will not apply where a public authority is exercising a statutory power and has no discretion as to whether or how to exercise that power, or no discretion as to how to perform its duties.

30.   Section 21B(2) defines "public authority" for the purposes of sections 21B, 21D and 21E. The definition is the same as that used in section 19B(2) of the RRA. It is also the same as the definition used in section 6(3)(b) of the Human Rights Act 1998. The definition is subject to the exceptions in new section 21B(3). It is also subject to the proviso in new section 21B(4), which specifies that a body will not be a public authority if the nature of the act being carried out is private. For example, the BBC would not be considered to be a public authority when carrying out its commercial activities.

31.   Section 21B(5) provides a regulation-making power that will allow for specified public authorities to be exempted from the prohibition of discrimination in section 21B(1).

32.   Section 21B(7) sets the boundaries between the new public authority duty in section 21B(1) and the other provisions of the DDA. The intention is, in broad terms, that where something is unlawful under another provision of the DDA, that other provision, and not section 21B(1), will apply. This principle applies in the same way where something would be unlawful but for the operation of any other provision of the DDA or regulations made under it (for example, a proviso or an exception). So where, for example, a public authority is an employer or a service provider, its acts as an employer or as a service provider will be governed by the existing DDA provisions relevant to that sphere of activity (Part 2 in the case of employment, sections 19 to 21 in the case of the provision of services). It will not also be liable, as a public authority, for the same acts under section 21B(1).

33.   Section 21B(8) creates an exception, for the case of office holders, to the general principle set out by section 21B(7). Under certain conditions and where sections 4C to 4E do not apply to appointment to the office or post in question, section 21B(1) will apply both to the function of appointing and to other functions of the public authority vis-à-vis the holder of the office. An example might be the function of a local education authority when appointing a school governor, which is an office not covered by the terms of section 4C.

34.   Section 21B(9) creates, under certain conditions, a further exception to the general principle created by section 21B(7) for the case of certain elected office or post holders. Under certain conditions and where sections 4C to 4E do not apply to appointment to the office or post in question, section 21B(1) will apply to functions of a public authority in relation to a candidate or prospective candidate for certain public offices or posts and to functions of the authority vis-à-vis the elected office holder once he holds office. This means, for example, that functions of a local education authority in organising an election of parent school governors would be covered by section 21B(1). The election itself is not a function of a public authority and is not covered by section 21B(1). The functions of the public authority in relation to the parent governor, once elected, would also be covered by section 21B(1).

New section 21C: Exceptions from section 21B(1)

35.   New section 21C sets out a number of functions to which section 21B(1) will not apply. New section 21C(1), (2) and (3) provide exemptions from section 21B(1) for judicial and legislative acts. There is also an exemption in new section 21C(4) concerning the institution of criminal proceedings.

36.   There is a regulation-making power in new section 21C(5) which will allow other functions to be exempted from the effect of the prohibition of discrimination in new section 21B(1).

New section 21D: Meaning of "discrimination"

37.   New section 21D defines the meaning of discrimination for the purposes of section 21B(1). The definition of discrimination mirrors, insofar as it is possible to do so, the definition of discrimination used for service providers in section 20 of the DDA.

38.   There are two forms of discrimination. The first form is set out in new section 21D(1) and is the less favourable treatment of a disabled person for a reason related to his disability, where the public authority cannot show that the treatment in question is justified under section 21D(3), (5) or (7)(c).

39.   The second form of discrimination is set out in new section 21D(2). In order for this sort of discrimination to be proved, an individual must show that, to his or her detriment, the public authority has failed to comply with a duty imposed by new section 21E, and the authority must be unable to show that its failure is justified under new section 21D(3), (5) or (7)(c).

New section 21D(3) to (5): Justification

40.   New section 21D(3) to (5) deal with the way in which a public authority may justify treatment or a failure to comply with the section 21E duty that indicates a prima facie breach of section 21D(1) or 21D(2).

41.   New section 21D(5) sets out one possible justification: the public authority concerned must show that the treatment, or failure to comply with the section 21E duty, is a proportionate means of achieving a legitimate aim. It is envisaged that a

public authority will be able to rely on this justification only in relation to matters of public interest (for example, the detection of crime) that, subject to an assessment of proportionality, can be said to be sufficiently important to override the right conferred by new section 21B(1). There is a regulation-making power in new section 21D(7)(b) to provide that this justification should not apply in certain circumstances and to amend or remove the justification. In connection with this power, see also the new section 67(3A) inserted by paragraph 33(4) of Schedule 1.

42. New section 21D(4) sets out further conditions of justification. A public authority has to satisfy the requirements of new section 21D(3) in order to justify the discriminatory treatment or failure.

43. A public authority must first show that it holds the opinion that one or more of the conditions set out in section 21D(4) is satisfied. These conditions concern: health and safety (new section 21D(4)(a)); incapacity to give consent (new section 21D(4)(b)); and protecting the rights and freedoms of others (new section 21D(4)(d)). There is also a justification relating to extra costs (new section 21D(4)(c)) that is available only in relation to less favourable treatment discrimination, as defined in section 21D(1).

44. Once a public authority proves that it holds the opinion that one of these conditions is satisfied, it must then show – on the basis of new section 21D(3)(b) – that it is reasonable, in all the circumstances of the case, for it to hold that opinion. If both of the steps in new section 21D(3) are satisfied, then the public authority can justify the less favourable treatment or failure to comply with the section 21E duty.

45. New section 21D(6) contains a regulation-making power in relation to the public authority's assessment of justification for its acts. This power would allow the Secretary of State to stipulate the circumstances in which it is or is not reasonable for the public authority to hold the opinion mentioned in subsection (3)(a). The regulation-making power will apply in relation to a public authority's ability to justify less favourable treatment or a failure to comply with the reasonable adjustment duty: the power will allow circumstances to be stipulated in which it is, and is not, reasonable for a public authority to hold the opinion that a condition of justification applies.

46. New section 21D(7)(a) provides a regulation-making power to amend, or remove, a condition of justification listed in new section 21D(4), or to make provision for a justification not to apply in specified circumstances. New section 21D(7)(b) is mentioned in the note on new section 21D(5) above. New section 21D(7)(c) gives a regulation-making power to add new justifications to those already existing in new section 21D(3) to (5).

New section 21E: Making of adjustments by public authorities

47. New section 21E imposes, on public authorities carrying out functions, duties equivalent to those imposed on service providers by section 21 of the DDA. In broad terms, new section 21E puts public authorities under a duty to make reasonable adjustments for disabled persons (such as adjustments to procedures,

alterations to the physical features of buildings or the provision of an auxiliary service such as a BSL interpreter), where such persons are – by reason of their disability – disadvantaged in some way by, or in relation to, the carrying-out of the function. The duty requires public authorities to anticipate the requirements of disabled persons and the adjustments that may need to be made for them.

48.   For the purposes of this section, two different aspects of public functions are considered separately:

- First, the possibility that the exercise of a function may confer benefits on people affected by the exercise of the function. For example, that would be the case where a local authority is making grants to members of the public. In these cases, the provisions require public authorities to make reasonable adjustments when failing to make such an adjustment would make it 'impossible or unreasonably difficult' for a disabled person to receive such a benefit.

- Second, the possibility that the exercise of a function may subject people affected by its exercise to a detriment. For example, that would be the case where a law enforcement agency exercises a power to arrest or detain members of the public. In these cases, the provisions require public authorities to make reasonable adjustments in order to avoid making it 'unreasonably adverse' for disabled people to experience being subjected to the detriment.

49.   The so-called trigger for the duty to make a reasonable adjustment will therefore depend on whether the carrying-out of the function is capable of conferring a benefit or subjecting a person to a detriment.

50.   When the relevant trigger is met, new section 21E(1) and (2) places a duty on a public body to take reasonable steps to change policies, practices or procedures (such as waiving a requirement in certain circumstances to fill out a form in writing). This duty is analogous to section 21(1) of the DDA.

51.   When the relevant trigger is met, new section 21E(3) and (4) places a duty on a public body to take reasonable steps to deal with a physical feature (for example, installing a ramp as an alternative to steps). This duty is analogous to section 21(2) of the DDA.

52.   New section 21E(5)(a) allows regulations to prescribe matters that can be taken into account when deciding whether the means of avoiding a physical feature (new section 21E(4)(c)) or an alternative method of carrying out the function (new section 21E(4)(d)) is reasonable. New section 21E(5)(b) gives a regulation-making power to allow categories of public bodies to be specified to which the duty to make reasonable adjustments to physical features in section 21E(4) does not apply.

53.   When the relevant trigger is met, new section 21E(6) and (7) places a duty on public authorities to take reasonable steps to provide auxiliary aids or services (such

as notification of a decision on audio tape). This duty is intended to be analogous to section 21(4) of the DDA.

54.　New section 21E(10) makes it clear that a breach of a duty imposed by section 21E is not actionable as such. Rather the duties are for the purposes of determining whether a public body has discriminated against a disabled person for the purposes of section 21B(1).

Section 3: Duties of Public Authorities

55.　This section amends the DDA by inserting a new Part 5A following section 49. The effect of this is to introduce into the DDA provisions which impose on public authorities duties relating to disabled people that are similar to those imposed by section 71 of the Race Relations Act 1976 (as substituted by the Race Relations (Amendment) Act 2000, section 2).

56.　The new Part 5A is intended to ensure that bodies which exercise public functions "mainstream" disability rights issues when exercising those functions. This means, in broad terms, that public bodies, when making decisions, or when developing or implementing a new policy, must make consideration of the needs of disabled people an integral part of the policy-making or decision-making process with a view to eliminating discrimination and harassment and to improving opportunities for, and promoting positive attitudes towards, disabled people. In addition, when exercising functions, bodies must take account of the need to encourage disabled people to take part in public life.

New section 49A: General Duty

57.　New section 49A(1) sets out the six prongs of the duty. It requires a public authority, as defined in section 49B, to have due regard, when carrying out its functions, to the need to eliminate unlawful discrimination against disabled people, the need to eliminate disability-related harassment of disabled people, the need to improve equality of opportunity for disabled people, the need to promote positive attitudes towards disabled people, and the need to encourage participation by disabled people in public life. The duty will be enforceable through judicial review.

58.　New section 49A(1)(d) requires public authorities to have due regard to the need to take steps to take account of disabled persons' disabilities or, in effect, to have due regard to the need to take steps to overcome the effects of disabilities. This underlines that 'equality of opportunity' cannot be achieved simply by treating disabled and non-disabled people alike, and recognises the long-standing principle that it is sometimes necessary to take positive steps to overcome the barriers faced by disabled people by making reasonable adjustments (such as providing information in different formats) or by making special provision for disabled people's needs (such as providing specialist transport services when public transport is inaccessible).

59.　New section 49A(2) makes it clear that compliance with the general duty in section 49A(1) will not detract from a public authority's obligations to comply with other provisions of the DDA.

New section 49B: Meaning of "public authority" in Part 5A

60.　New section 49B(1) defines "public authority" for the purposes of section 49A. The definition in new section 49B(1)(a) is the same as the definition used in new section 21B(2) (to be inserted by section 2).

61.　The definition of "public authority" in new section 49B(1)(a) is also the same as that used in section 6(3)(b) of the Human Rights Act 1998. It is subject to the proviso in new section 49B(2), which provides that a body will not be a public authority if the nature of the act being carried out is private. For example, the Law Society is likely to be covered in respect of its statutory functions such as those relating to the regulation of solicitors, but not its private functions - for example the representation of the interests of the profession in dealings with Government.

62.　The list of bodies subject to the equivalent race duties (see Schedule 1A to the Race Relations Act 1976, as inserted by the Race Relations (Amendment) Act 2000) was compiled with regard to the Human Rights Act definition of "public authority", and so it is expected that the range of bodies covered by the definition in new section 49B will be similar. The definition will certainly include Government Departments, local authorities, the police and other governmental organisations.

63.　New section 49B(1)(b) excludes certain bodies from the definition of public authority, in particular the Scottish Parliament and the bodies listed in section 21B(3) (see section 2), for example the Houses of Parliament and the intelligence agencies.

64.　New section 49B(3) provides a power, by regulations, to exclude certain bodies from the definition of public authority for the purposes of Part 5A. It could be used, for example, to clarify the situation where there was doubt as to whether a body was covered or not, or to exclude bodies altogether where there were good policy reasons as to why they should not be covered by the section 49A(1) duty.

New section 49C: Exceptions from section 49A(1)

65.　New section 49C(1) to (3) set out certain acts which are not subject to the duties in section 49A(1) such as judicial acts, legislative acts, and acts relating to employment in the armed forces.

66.　New section 49C(4) provides a power to define in regulations other acts in relation to which duties under section 49A(1) will not apply. This would enable, for example, regulations to clarify the situation where there was doubt as to whether an act was covered or not, or to exclude particular types of act from those duties where there would be good policy reasons as to why they should not be covered.

New section 49D: Power to impose specific duties

67.　New section 49D(1) to (4) will provide powers for the Secretary of State, in respect of all bodies other than certain Scottish bodies, and for the Scottish

Ministers in respect of those Scottish bodies, to impose by regulations specific duties on bodies to assist the bodies in the performance of their duties under section 49A(1). Such duties may involve, for example, some organisations having to produce disability equality schemes, or carry out certain types of monitoring.

68. In the case of cross-border public authorities (within the meaning of section 88(5) of the Scotland Act 1998), the Secretary of State may impose, by regulations, duties in respect of their functions which are not Scottish functions, and the Scottish Ministers may impose, by regulations, duties in respect of their Scottish functions. New section 49D(8) requires that, before placing cross-border public authorities under specific duties, the Secretary of State must consult the Scottish Ministers. Similarly, new section 49D(9) requires that, before placing cross-border public authorities under specific duties, the Scottish Ministers must consult the Secretary of State.

69. New section 49D(5) to (7) provide for other consultation requirements in relation to regulations under section 49D(1) to (4).

New section 49E: Compliance notices

70. New section 49E sets out the framework for the enforcement of specific duties imposed by regulations under new section 49D. The Disability Rights Commission may serve a compliance notice on a public authority where it is satisfied that the authority is not complying with any specific duty imposed by such regulations. A compliance notice would require the public authority to comply with the duty concerned and also to inform the Disability Rights Commission of the steps it has taken (or is taking) to do so. It could also require the public authority to give the Disability Rights Commission other information that may be required in order to verify that the duty has been complied with.

New section 49F: Enforcement of compliance notices

71. New section 49F contains provisions about the enforcement of compliance notices. New section 49F(1) and (2) enable the Disability Rights Commission to apply to a county court, or in the case of Scotland a sheriff court, for an order to supply information where it believes that a public authority has not provided, or intends not to provide, information requested under section 49E, and for the court to grant such an order where the relevant conditions are met.

72. New section 49F(3) and (4) enable the Disability Rights Commission, at the end of the time specified in a compliance notice issued under section 49E, to apply to a county court, or in the case of Scotland a sheriff court, for an order that the public authority concerned must comply with a duty imposed by regulations made under new section 49D. The court has powers to grant such an order where it is satisfied that the duty has not been complied with.

73. New section 49F(5) makes it clear that the only sanctions for not complying with a duty under section 49D are those set out in sections 49E and 49F.

Section 4: Police

74.   Section 4 amends section 64A of the DDA (inserted into the DDA with effect from 1 October 2004 by the Amendment Regulations) so as to insert provisions analogous to those contained in section 76A(4) to (6) of the Race Relations Act 1976 (as inserted by the Race Relations (Amendment) Act 2000, section 4).   As amended by section 4, section 64A will set out who the correct defendant is in the case of a claim of discrimination being made against a police officer under Part 3 of the DDA (for example, where it is alleged that a police officer has discriminated against a disabled person when carrying out a function). The section also authorises payment from the police fund of compensation or of costs of settlement in relation to such a claim.

Section 5: Application of sections 19 to 21 of the 1995 Act to transport vehicles

75.   Section 5 inserts a new section 21ZA into the DDA. Paragraph 13(3) of Schedule 1 removes the existing exclusion of transport services from sections 19 to 21 of the DDA. This is replaced by the more precise exclusion in new section 21ZA(1) and (2), i.e. one relating only to transport services consisting of the provision and use of a vehicle. Section 21ZA(3) then confers a regulation-making power to enable such services to be brought within the scope of those sections (which make it unlawful to discriminate against a disabled person in the provision of goods, facilities and services). This will enable those sections to be applied in whole or in part to different transport vehicles at different times.

76.   Section 21ZA(1) excludes, subject to section 21ZA(3), transport services which involve the provision or use of a vehicle from the provisions of section 19(1)(a), (c) or (d) of the DDA. Under section 21ZA(1)(a), discrimination is excluded if it arises through the provision, or non-provision, of a vehicle. Under section 21ZA(1)(b), discrimination is excluded if it arises through the provision, or non-provision, of services to a person whilst travelling in a vehicle. This would, for example, apply to the sale of tickets on board a train.

77.   Section 21ZA(2) excludes, subject to section 21ZA(3), transport services which involve the provision or use of a vehicle from the provisions of section 21(1), (2) and (4) of the DDA (duty to provide adjustments). It specifies that it will not be reasonable for the service provider to have to take steps which would involve altering or removing a physical feature of a transport vehicle. It also specifies that it will not be reasonable to require a transport operator to have to take steps affecting whether vehicles are provided or what type of vehicle is provided, or to have to take steps affecting the services provided within a vehicle.

78.   Section 21ZA(3) provides a power to make regulations to disapply the exclusion in sections 21ZA(1) and (2). This power will enable the exclusion to be lifted in respect of different types of vehicle at different times. Furthermore, it will enable the exclusion to be lifted for particular types of service within generic modes of transport at different times. For example, the exclusion could be lifted for all public transport vehicles at a particular time, but applied to aviation and marine vehicles at a later date if considered necessary.

Section 6: Rail vehicles: application of accessibility regulations

79.   Section 46 in Part 5 of the DDA gives the Secretary of State power to make rail vehicle accessibility regulations ("RVAR") for the purposes of securing that it is possible for disabled persons to get on and off regulated rail vehicles in safety and without unreasonable difficulty, and to be carried in such vehicles in safety and in reasonable comfort. Section 6(1) inserts a new sub-section (4A) into section 46, the effect of which is to require the Secretary of State to exercise the power in section 46(1) to make accessibility regulations so as to ensure that all rail vehicles are regulated, i.e. subject to provisions of the RVAR, no later than 1st January 2020. This requirement does not disturb the power under section 46(5) of the DDA under which RVAR may make different provision for different vehicles, the same types of vehicles used in different circumstances, or in different circumstances. Neither does it affect the power under section 47(1) to exempt vehicles from requirements of RVAR or prevent such orders being made or having effect after 1st January 2020.

80.   Section 46(6) defines a "rail vehicle" for the purposes of the section as a vehicle "constructed or adapted to carry passengers on any railway, tramway or prescribed system; and first brought into use, or belonging to a class of vehicle first brought into use, after 31st December 1998". Section 6(2) replaces this definition by removing the second part of it, so that there is no 'start date'. This change enables the Secretary of State to achieve his policy objective of applying RVAR to rail vehicles first brought into use before 1st January 1999, and also to newer vehicles which are of the same type as ones first used before RVAR came into force on 1st January 1999. This change of definition will enable the Secretary of State to set the date in RVAR by which time all rail vehicles must comply with requirements of the regulations, although that date may not be later than 1st January 2020. Together with the power in the existing section 46(5), it also means that the Secretary of State can provide for RVAR to apply to rail vehicles which are not currently regulated (i.e. not subject to RVAR) when they are refurbished, and prescribe the extent to which they must conform.

81.   Section 6(3) replaces existing section 47(1) of the DDA. Section 47(1) currently allows the Secretary of State to make exemption orders, authorising regulated rail vehicles to be used for carriage even though they do not comply with requirements of the RVAR which they are required to comply with. The new provision continues to allow the Secretary of State to make exemption orders in respect of regulated rail vehicles, but clarifies the law by specifically allowing exemptions from the operational requirements of RVAR as well as construction requirements. As well as restating the power to exempt the use of any rail vehicle of a specified description, or the use of any rail vehicle in specified circumstances, it expressly confers power to exempt the use of vehicles of a specified description in specified circumstances. So, for example, all the vehicles used on a particular railway, for example a heritage railway, could be exempted from some or all of the requirements of the RVAR.

82.   New section 67(5A), which is inserted into the DDA by paragraph 33 of

Schedule 1, provides that exemption orders made under section 47(1) of the DDA may, at the discretion of the Secretary of State, be subject to either the draft affirmative or the negative resolution procedure. Section 6(4) inserts new section 67A into the DDA, which sets out the procedure for the exercise of this discretion. New section 67A(3) empowers the Secretary of State to make regulations setting out the criteria for the exercise of this discretion. The Secretary of State is required to consult the Disabled Persons Transport Advisory Committee, and other appropriate bodies, before making such regulations, which will be subject to the draft affirmative procedure. Until regulations made under new section 67A(3) are in force, exemption orders made under section 47(1) of the DDA will be subject to the draft affirmative resolution procedure. This will give greater parliamentary scrutiny over the making of exemption orders under section 47(1).

83. Section 6(5) inserts new section 67B into the DDA to require the Secretary of State to produce an annual report on rail vehicle exemption orders. The report will be produced for each calendar year, and must contain details of exemption orders made under section 47(1). It must also contain information about the consultation on both applications for exemption orders and the exercise of the discretion as to whether such orders should be subject to the negative or affirmative resolution procedure. The report may also include other information, for example, information about applications for exemption which have been rejected or only granted in part. The report is required to be laid before both Houses of Parliament.

Section 7: Rail vehicles: accessibility compliance certificates
84. This section inserts new sections 47A to 47C into the DDA, the effect of which will be to require prescribed rail vehicles to have a rail vehicle accessibility compliance certificate. It is intended that the requirement to have a certificate will apply to all new rail vehicles and vehicles that are refurbished. It also makes consequential amendments to sections 49 of the DDA (forgery and false statements) and 68(1) of the DDA (interpretation). The effect of these new sections, and corresponding changes to existing provisions, is to set up a RVAR certification scheme. The provisions include power for the Secretary of State to make regulations providing for the appointment of independent assessors who will be responsible for checking regulated rail vehicles for compliance against each RVAR requirement to which that vehicle is required to conform. They also empower the Secretary of State to make regulations setting out the procedure for obtaining certificates, including provisions for assessors to charge fees, and a mechanism for disputes between assessors and applicants for certificates to be referred to the Secretary of State. It is expected that for most rail vehicles (excluding trams and light rail systems) the RVAR compliance assessment will generally be carried out by the 'notified bodies' with responsibility for assessing vehicles under the high speed interoperability regime (Directive 96/48/EC, implemented by S.I. 2002/1166). The assessment of vehicles for RVAR compliance will be an integral part of the work of notified bodies in checking against the technical standards applied under that Directive.

New section 47A: Rail vehicle accessibility compliance certificates
85. Section 47A(1) prohibits a regulated rail vehicle from being used for carriage unless a valid compliance certificate has been issued for that vehicle. It should be noted that this subsection applies only to   vehicles prescribed in regulations

made under subsection (2).

86.   Subsection (2) is a regulation-making power which enables the Secretary of State to prescribe vehicles which will require a certificate. If, as intended, the power is exercised to prescribe new rail vehicles and rail vehicles that are refurbished, the power will also enable regulations to set a date from which time those vehicles will have to be certified.

87.   Subsection (3) describes a rail vehicle accessibility compliance certificate. A certificate's purpose is to indicate that the Secretary of State is satisfied that a rail vehicle is compliant with those provisions of RVAR with which it is required to conform. The provisions with which vehicles are required to conform will be prescribed in the RVAR, including different requirements in the case of refurbished vehicles where, depending on the extent of the refurbishment work, not all the provisions may apply.

88.   Subsection (4) provides a general power to enable certificates to be made subject to conditions. For example, an operator could be required to inform the Secretary of State if there was a change in the operating company or if the vehicle was used on a different service.

89.   Subsections (5) and (6) make provision in respect of the refusal of the Secretary of State to issue a certificate. An applicant can ask the Secretary of State, within a timescale to be set in regulations, to review his decision. A fee can be charged for such a review. The Secretary of State must review the decision taking into account any written representations submitted by the applicant within the timescale set in regulations.

New section 47B: Rail vehicle accessibility compliance certificates: supplementary
90.   Section 47B(1) empowers the Secretary of State to make regulations with respect to compliance certificates, and other subsections set out examples of the provisions that may be included in such regulations. These relate in particular to the procedure relating to the application for and granting of certificates, and the conditions to which they may be made subject, together with provisions as to who may apply, and in what form.

91.   Subsection (3)(c) enables regulations to specify the information that is to accompany an application for a certificate. In particular, the regulations may require an application to be accompanied by a report of a compliance assessment. Subsection (4) defines a "compliance assessment" as being an assessment of a rail vehicle against those provisions of RVAR with which it is required to conform. Subsection (5) stipulates that the regulations may provide for such assessments to be carried out by a person appointed by the Secretary of State, known as an "appointed assessor".

92.   Subsection (6) applies in the event that regulations under subsection (1) do in fact require that an application for a certificate be accompanied by a report of a compliance assessment carried out by an appointed assessor. It provides that

regulations made under subsection (1) may include provisions about the appointment by the Secretary of State of appointed assessors and, under subsection (6)(b), the regulations may make provision for such assessors to charge fees in connection with their work in compiling a compliance assessment or a pre-assessment. Subsection (6)(d) requires the regulations to include provision for referral to the Secretary of State of any dispute between an appointed assessor and a person who requested a compliance assessment about what provisions of RVAR a vehicle should be assessed against or whether or not a vehicle complies with any particular requirement of RVAR.

93. Subsection (7) defines "compliance assessment" in subsection (6)(b) to (d) as including pre-assessment work, for example, giving an advance opinion on the final compliance of a new design feature. This will enable prospective applicants for compliance certificates to obtain a view from an appointed assessor as to the likely compliance of a particular design before embarking on the construction of the feature.

New section 47C: Rail vehicle accessibility compliance certificates: fees

94. Section 47C(1) empowers the Secretary of State to make regulations prescribing that fees should be charged for the carrying out of certain administrative tasks relating to the issuing of compliance certificates. Subsection (2) stipulates that any fees received by the Secretary of State under subsection (1) must be paid to the Consolidated Fund. Before making such regulations, the Secretary of State must consult representative organisations.

95. Section 7(2) inserts into section 49 of the DDA a new subsection (1)(e) and amends subsection (4). The effect of these amendments is to make it a criminal offence for a person, with intent to deceive, to forge, alter, use, lend, or allow another person to use a rail vehicle accessibility compliance certificate, or to make or have in his possession a document which resembles such a certificate. The amendment to section 49(4) makes it an offence to knowingly make a false statement in order to obtain a rail vehicle accessibility compliance certificate.

Section 8: Enforcement and penalties

96. Section 8(1) inserts new sections 47D to 47M into the DDA. The effect is to replace the criminal sanctions in existing section 46(3) and (4) for non-compliance with the RVAR (which are repealed – see paragraph 27(a) of Schedule 1) with a civil enforcement regime which enables penalties to be levied. The new sections will enable the Secretary of State to issue an operator with an improvement notice, which sets a deadline for a non-compliance to be rectified. If the non-compliance continues after the improvement deadline, a final notice can be issued. If the final deadline is missed the Secretary of State can impose a penalty. An operator can lodge an objection with the Secretary of State against either the imposition or level of a penalty. The provisions also provide a right of appeal to the court.

New section 47D: Penalty for using rail vehicle without accessibility compliance certificate

97.   New section 47D allows the Secretary of State to require an operator to pay a penalty if he uses a regulated rail vehicle that does not have a valid accessibility compliance certificate issued under section 47A to carry passengers. New sections 47J to 47L contain detailed provision about penalties.

New section 47E: Penalty for using rail vehicle that does not conform with accessibility regulations

98.   This section sets out the procedure to be followed by the Secretary of State in respect of an operator of a regulated rail vehicle which appears not to comply with the construction requirements of the RVAR. The procedure involves the issuing of two notices (an improvement notice and a final notice) and, if the vehicle is used despite still being non-compliant with the RVAR, the Secretary of State may impose a penalty. The various timescales leading up to the imposition of the penalty are to be set out in regulations, but the Government has suggested in consultation that the final notice period should be two weeks.

New section 47F: Penalty for using rail vehicle otherwise than in conformity with accessibility regulations

99.   This section makes similar provisions to section 47E but in respect of vehicles used in a way which does not comply with the operational, rather than technical, requirements of RVAR. This might apply, for example, where the vehicle has the appropriate equipment to assist a disabled person in getting on or off the vehicle, but no member of staff is available to operate it.

New section 47G: Sections 47E and 47F: inspection of rail vehicles

100.   This section sets out new powers of inspection, to be available where the Secretary of State has reasonable grounds for suspecting that a regulated rail vehicle does not conform with those provisions of RVAR with which it is required to conform. The section also grants similar powers of inspection following the issuing of notices under section 47E(1) or (4). The Secretary of State may authorise an 'inspector' to examine and test such vehicles and, for the purposes of exercising these powers, the inspector is empowered to enter premises at which he believes the vehicle to be kept, and to enter the vehicle. If an inspector is obstructed in the exercise of these powers the Secretary of State may, in certain circumstances, impose a penalty on the operator.

New section 47H: Sections 47E and 47F: supplementary powers

101.   Subsection (1) enables the Secretary of State to issue a notice to an operator requiring him to provide information by a specified deadline to enable a rail vehicle which is described in that notice to be identified. This may be necessary, for example, where a member of the public reports a technical breach of the RVAR and knows the time and route of the journey on which the vehicle was being used but not the vehicle's fleet number. Under subsection (3), the Secretary of State may impose a penalty on the recipient of a notice under subsection (1) if they fail to provide the information required by the deadline, which must be a minimum of 14

days from the date on which the notice is given.

New section 47J: Penalties under sections 47D to 47H: amount, due date and recovery

102.   This section sets out the detail in terms of amount, due date and recovery with regard to penalties imposed under sections 47D to 47H.   It stipulates that the maximum penalty cannot exceed the amount prescribed in regulations <u>and</u> that it also cannot exceed 10% of the turnover of the operator subject to the penalty. "Turnover", for the purposes of subsection (2), must be determined in accordance with provisions set out in regulations. Subsection (5) enables the Secretary of State to start court proceedings to recover any penalty payable to him.

103.   Subsection (8) requires the Secretary of State to issue a code of practice setting out matters that will be considered in determining the level of a penalty. For example, the code could specify a sliding scale of penalty levels so that a first 'offence' warranted a lower penalty. The Secretary of State is required to take account of the code when imposing a penalty under these provisions, as is a court in considering an appeal against the penalty under sections 47L: see section 47L(3). Before issuing either the first or a revised code, the Secretary of State must lay a draft before Parliament.

New section 47K: Penalties under sections 47D to 47H: procedure

104.   This section sets out the procedure for the imposition of penalties under sections 47D to 47H.   Subsections (4) and (5) set out the operator's right to object to a penalty either because he does not think he is liable for such a penalty, or because he thinks the amount is too high. The Secretary of State is then under an obligation to consider the objection and take appropriate action.

New section 47L: Penalties under sections 47D to 47H: appeals

105.   This section sets out the right of an operator subject to a penalty under these provisions to appeal to a court on the grounds that either they are not liable to a penalty, or that the level is too high. An appeal under this section is a re-hearing of the Secretary of State's original decision to impose a penalty and may be brought whether or not the operator has given a notice of objection under section 47K(4), or the Secretary of State has already reduced a penalty.

New section 47M: Sections 46 to 47H: interpretation

106.   Subsection (1) defines an "operator" for the purposes of sections 46 to 47H as the person having the management of a rail vehicle, and subsection (2) defines, for the purposes of sections 46 to 47H, the use of a vehicle for carriage as use for the carriage of passengers. The existing definitions of these terms in section 46 of the DDA are repealed under Schedule 2 to the 2005 Act.

107. Subsection (3) provides that where an exemption order under section 47 is in place, the references in sections 47A to 47G to the provisions of RVAR with which the vehicle is required to conform do not include a provision in respect of which an exemption order has been made.

108. *Section 8(2)* inserts into section 49 of the DDA a new subsection (5) making it a criminal offence for a person to impersonate an inspector authorised by the Secretary of State for the purposes of section 47G.

Section 9: Recognition of disabled persons' badges issued outside Great Britain

109. This section amends the Chronically Sick and Disabled Persons Act 1970 ("CSDPA 1970") which established the disabled persons' parking badge ("blue badge") scheme. This scheme provides for certain parking concessions to operate in favour of disabled people whose vehicles display blue badges. This section (which extends to England and Wales only) introduces new sections 21A to 21C into CSDPA 1970. The principal effect of the new provisions is to provide that the holders of foreign disabled persons' badges be afforded the same concessions as holders of domestic "blue badges" in respect of parking concessions. The section makes provision to formalise existing (non-statutory) recognition of parking badges issued in the EU or in certain other European countries (for which there is reciprocal recognition), and to extend this recognition to badges issued in other countries.

New section 21A of CSDPA 1970: Recognition of badges issued outside Great Britain

110. New section 21A provides for the recognition of non-GB disabled persons' badges ("recognised badges"). Disabled persons' badges issued in Northern Ireland (new section 21A(1)(a)) will be recognised badges, as will badges issued under those provisions of foreign laws which the Secretary of State (for England) and the National Assembly (for Wales) will specify in regulations. Such regulations will also provide for the manner in which a recognised badge must be displayed (new section 21A(3)).

111. Section 21A(4) to (9) make provision in respect of non-GB recognised badges corresponding to existing provisions in respect of British blue badges. These provisions are intended to criminalise, and aid the detection of, the fraudulent use of purportedly genuine badges. The offence in new section 21A(4) mirrors section 21(4E) of CSDPA 1970 which relates to domestic badges. The power to inspect recognised badges (in section 21A(6)) and the following, consequential, subsections mirror the power and provisions in respect of British blue badges contained in section 94 of the Traffic Management Act 2004.

New section 21B of CSDPA 1970: Recognised badges treated as badges under section 21 for certain purposes

112. New section 21B provides for, or enables, concessions which currently apply in respect of GB blue badges to apply in respect of recognised badges. Those concessions may be concessions in or by virtue of local authority orders which would otherwise restrict parking or waiting (to which orders, among others, section 21B(2)(a) relates), or orders designating parking places for the use of disabled people (to which orders, among others, section 21B(2)(b) relates).

113. New section 21B(3) will enable this equality of treatment between GB and recognised badge holders to be extended for such other purposes as may be prescribed: this may extend to provisions which grant concessions in respect of road

use as well as those which grant concessions in respect of parking.

New section 21C of CSDPA 1970: Sections 21A and 21B: regulations and interpretation

114.   This new section contains provision supplementary to the various regulation-making powers conferred on the Secretary of State or National Assembly for Wales by new sections 21A and 21B.

115.   Note that Part 2 of Schedule 1 (the effects of which are explained below in the context of the notes to that Schedule) makes minor or consequential changes pursuant to the recognition of non-GB badges.

Section 10: Discriminatory advertisements

116.   Section 16B was inserted into the DDA by regulation 15(1) of the Amendment Regulations. This provision makes it unlawful for employers and others covered by Part 2 of the DDA (employment field) to publish or cause to be published a discriminatory advertisement inviting applications for a job, training or other relevant benefit.   Section 17B of the DDA (as inserted by the Amendment Regulations) provides for enforcement of section 16B.   It confers powers on the Disability Rights Commission to seek a declaration from an employment tribunal and, in some circumstances, to apply to a county court for an injunction (or, in Scotland, to a sheriff court for an interdict).

117.   As it currently stands, section 16B(1) does not prohibit third parties (such as newspapers) from publishing discriminatory advertisements on behalf of the person placing the advertisement. In order to fill this gap, section 10(2) replaces section 16B(1) with new subsection (1), which extends the scope of the prohibition to cover third party publishers who publish a discriminatory advertisement on behalf of another. (It also makes it clear that section 16B applies so that it covers advertisements which indicate an intention to discriminate against a person who has had a disability, as well as a person who has a disability.)

118.   New subsection (2A), as inserted by section 10(3), exempts a third party publisher from liability under subsection (1) if he can prove that, in publishing the advertisement, he relied on a statement made by the person who placed the advertisement (such as an employer) to the effect that publication of the advertisement would not be unlawful, and that it was reasonable for him to rely on that statement.

119.   New subsection (2B) makes it an offence for a person knowingly or recklessly to make a false or misleading statement about the lawfulness of an advertisement as described in new subsection (2A). The offence carries a fine not exceeding level 5 on the standard scale (currently £5000) on summary conviction.

Section 11: Group insurance

120.   Section 11(1) repeals the provisions concerning group insurance schemes presently contained in Part 2 of the DDA, section 18.   That section applies where a

provider of insurance services (for example, a medical expenses insurer) enters into arrangements with an employer under which the employer's employees receive services provided by that insurer. The effect of section 18 is that an act of discrimination by such an insurer against a disabled employee is treated as discrimination falling within Part 2 of the DDA, where the act would be unlawful under Part 3 of the DDA if the service concerned were to be provided to the employee as a member of the public. (Sections 19 to 21 of Part 3 make it unlawful for a service provider to discriminate in certain circumstances as regards the provision of goods, facilities or services to the public or a section of the public.) The practical effect of section 18 is that cases to which it applies are dealt with by the employment tribunal.

121.   It is considered that section 18 is unnecessary and confusing. Following the repeal of the section, it will be clear that a person who provides group insurance services to employees of particular employers would be regarded as a "provider of services[5]" for the purposes of sections 19 to 21, and consequently liable for an act of discrimination contrary to section 19(1) which they may commit against disabled persons employed by those employers. (An act of discrimination by an employer in relation to a group insurance scheme, e.g. refusing for discriminatory reasons to permit a disabled employee to have access to the scheme, will fall within Part 2 of the DDA, sections 4 and 4A – as substituted by the Amendment Regulations.)

122.   Section 11(2) inserts a new subsection (6A) into section 25 (enforcement, remedies and procedure) of the DDA. This new subsection ensures that claims of discrimination against an insurer concerning the provision of group insurance services are not subject to the Part 3 procedures and remedies set out in section 25 of the DDA – under which a victim of discrimination may bring proceedings in the county court or sheriff court claiming damages, an injunction or other relief. The provision should be read with paragraph 21 of Schedule 1, which amends section 25(8) to ensure that employment tribunals will have jurisdiction to consider such claims.

123.   Subsection (3) inserts a definition of group insurance arrangements into section 68(1) (interpretation) of the DDA. This goes a little wider than the definition currently in section 18(3) in that it covers all types of group insurance schemes, not just those relating to: termination of service; retirement, old age or death; or accident, injury, sickness or invalidity.

Section 12: Private clubs etc.
124.   Under the DDA, private members' clubs (referred to as "associations" in the new provisions) are not prohibited from discriminating against their members. Associations are only prevented from discriminating against disabled people in their capacity as employers (under Part 2 of the DDA) or providers of services to members of the public (under Part 3 of the DDA).

---

[5] A person is "a provider of services" for the purposes of sections 19 to 21 if he is concerned with the provision, in the United Kingdom, of services to the public or a section of the public: see section 19(2)(b).

125.   Section 12 inserts new sections 21F to 21J into Part 3 of the DDA and will make it unlawful for associations with 25 or more members to discriminate against disabled members, applicants for membership, associates and guests in certain circumstances. (The new sections are modelled on the provisions of section 25 of the Race Relations Act 1976.) As with other provisions in Part 3 of the DDA, a victim of discrimination contrary to new sections 21F to 21J could bring enforcement proceedings under section 25.

126.   Section 21F applies to any incorporated or unincorporated association with 25 or more members where admission to membership is regulated by its constitution (which may be written or oral) and is so conducted that its members do not constitute a section of the general public (section 21F(1)). In practice, this last requirement means that an association must operate a genuine policy of membership selection based on personal criteria so as to distinguish between members of the association and members of the public. Examples of a club which would be covered by this new section 21F include a golf club or a gentlemen's club, to which applicants for membership are required to make a personal application, be sponsored by other members as to their good character and then go through some kind of selection process, such as voting by existing members. A club which does not operate such a policy of membership selection is already covered by sections 19 to 21 of the DDA where it provides services to the public or a section of the public (whether for profit or not). Examples here would include social clubs, where payment of the requisite membership fee is all that is required to secure admittance to membership.

127.   New section 21F(2) to (5) set out the circumstances in which an act of discrimination by an association will be unlawful against the following: an applicant for membership (new subsection (2)); a member or associate of the association (new subsection (3)): a guest of the association (new subsection (4)); and an intended guest of the association (new subsection (5)).

128.   New subsection (2) protects a disabled applicant for membership from discrimination in relation to a refusal by a club to admit him as a member or the terms on which membership is granted.

129.   New subsection (3) prohibits discrimination against a disabled member (as defined in new section 21J(1)(a)) or a disabled associate (as defined in new section 21J(1)(b)) in the following ways: in relation to the way in which he is granted access to a benefit, facility or service provided by the club; where he is refused access to a benefit, facility or service; where he is deprived of membership or his rights as an associate; where his terms of membership or rights as an associate are varied; or where he is subjected to any other detriment.

130.   New subsection (4) prohibits discrimination by an association against a disabled guest (as defined in new section 21J(2)): in the way in which he is afforded access to a benefit, facility or service provided by the club; where he is refused access to a benefit, facility or service; or where he is subjected to any other

detriment.

131.   New subsection (5) prevents an association from discriminating against a disabled person where the association (or one of its members or associates) intends to invite him to be a guest of the association. It does so by making it unlawful for an association to discriminate against a disabled person: in the terms on which it is prepared to invite him or permit him to be invited by a member or associate to be a guest of the association; by refusing or deliberately omitting to invite him to be a guest; or by refusing to grant a member or associate permission to invite him as a guest.

132.   New subsection (5) will ensure that an association cannot avoid liability for discriminating against a disabled person by omitting to invite him, or by refusing or withdrawing an invitation by one of its members or associates, to an event to which he would have been invited but for his disability. For example, a decision by an association refusing to allow a member to invite his disabled wife to attend an annual dinner held by the association which was open to all members' spouses, because she was a wheelchair user, would be caught by new subsection (5).

133.   New section 21F(6) would make it unlawful for an association to discriminate against a disabled person by failing to comply with any duty to make reasonable adjustments imposed on the association by regulations made under section 21H (as to which, see the commentary below).

134.   New section 21G sets out the meaning of discrimination. Under new section 21G, unlawful discrimination for the purposes of new section 21F is defined as less favourable treatment of a disabled person for a disability-related reason in circumstances in which that treatment cannot be justified.   Less favourable treatment will only be capable of justification under new section 21G(2) where the association holds the opinion that one of the conditions in new section 21G(3) is satisfied, and it is reasonable for it to hold that opinion.

135.   The conditions set out in new section 21G(3) broadly correspond to those found in section 20(4) of the DDA in relation to service providers, but have been adapted to suit the circumstances of private clubs. Subsection (4) provides that any cost of affording a disabled person access to a benefit, facility or service which results from a duty under section 21H shall be disregarded for the purposes of subsection (3)(e), (f) and (g). Under new subsection (5), the Secretary of State may, by regulations, add to, amend or omit any of the conditions set out in new subsection (3) or provide for them not to apply in prescribed circumstances. This power is intended to enable the Secretary of State to adapt the conditions, should this prove necessary, following consultation.

136.   New section 21G(6) provides that an association also discriminates against a disabled person if it fails to comply with a duty to make adjustments imposed on it by new section 21H and it cannot show that such a failure is justified. New section 21H(1) and (2) enable the Secretary of State to make regulations prescribing the circumstances in which associations will be under a duty to make reasonable

adjustments (which could include the alteration of physical features or the provision of an auxiliary aid). The first exercise of that regulation-making power will be subject to the affirmative resolution procedure (see paragraph 33(5) of Schedule 1 described below).

137.   As the Secretary of State is consulting ("Consultation on private clubs; premises; the definition of disability and the questions procedure", December 2004, Cm 6402) before imposing such duties, the 2005 Act's provisions set out only the framework of this duty. It is not expected that the duties to be imposed by regulations made under new section 21H will go further than those which providers of goods, services or facilities are under by reason of section 21 of the DDA. In addition, it is expected that regulations will make provision for failure to make a reasonable adjustment to be justified in circumstances corresponding to circumstances set out in new section 21G(3).

138.   New section 21J defines "member", "associate" and "guest" for the purposes of sections 21F to 21H. A member is a person who belongs to the association by virtue of his admission to membership as provided for by its constitution. An associate is defined as a person who, although not a member of the association, has some or all of the rights enjoyed by members under its constitution.

139.   Subsection (2) provides that a guest of an association includes a person who is invited by a member or associate of the association with the permission of the association. The following are examples of persons who might be considered to be guests of an association: a disabled partner of a member invited to a club's annual dinner or other festive occasion; a member's adult son who has a severe learning disability and who joins his parents for a drink in a social club on a Saturday night. It is not intended to include a person who is invited onto the premises by the association in the course of their trade, such as a food and drink delivery-van driver or a plumber.

140.   Subsection (3) enables the Secretary of State to make regulations setting out the circumstances in which a person is to be treated as being, or not to be treated as being, a guest of the association for the purposes of sections 21F to 21H. The power might be used, for example, in the case of associations which operate over the Internet in order to define what is meant by a "guest" should this prove problematic in practice.

Section 13: discrimination in relation to letting of premises
141.   Disabled people are already protected against some forms of discrimination in relation to premises. The relevant provisions can be found in sections 22 to 24 of the DDA. Under those sections it is unlawful for persons who are selling or letting premises to discriminate against a disabled person in the way they offer to dispose of the premises to the disabled person, by refusing to offer to dispose of the premises to the disabled person, or in their treatment of him in relation to any waiting list for the premises. It is further unlawful for persons who manage premises to discriminate against a disabled person occupying the premises in the way they permit the disabled person to use any benefits or facilities, or by evicting

the disabled person or subjecting him to any other detriment. Provision is also made prohibiting discrimination where people withhold their licence or consent for the disposal of premises to a disabled person.

142.   Section 13 inserts new sections 24A to 24L into Part 3 of the DDA. These make it unlawful for landlords and managers, in relation to premises they wish to let or that are let, to discriminate against a disabled tenant or prospective tenant by failing without justification to comply with a duty to provide a reasonable adjustment for the disabled person.   As with other Part 3 provisions, a victim of discrimination contrary to new sections 24A to 24L will be able to bring enforcement proceedings in a county or sheriff court under section 25 of the DDA. See also new section 24M (premises provisions do not apply where other provisions operate) inserted by paragraph 20 of Schedule 1, discussed below, and section 16 (improvements to let dwelling houses).

143.   The letting of commercial and residential premises in the United Kingdom is covered. "Letting" is defined widely to include sub-letting – and the granting of contractual licences to occupy premises, i.e. where the legal relationship created is not one of landlord and tenant. (See new sections 24A(4) and 24G(4)).

144.   The new provisions would require a landlord or manager to take reasonable steps to change a policy, practice or procedure which makes it impossible or unreasonably difficult for—

- a disabled person to take a letting of the premises, or

- (where there is a letting already in existence) a disabled tenant – or other disabled person lawfully occupying the premises – to enjoy the premises or use a benefit or facility conferred with the lease,

so that the policy, practice or procedure concerned no longer has that effect (see new sections 24D and 24J(3) and (4)).

For example, a landlord or manager may be obliged (where it was reasonable to do so)—

- to allow a tenant who has mobility difficulties to leave his rubbish in another place if he cannot access the designated place;

- to allow an occupier who uses a wheelchair to use an existing accessible entrance at the back of a block of flats even though other tenants cannot use it.

145.   The provisions would also require a landlord or manager to take reasonable steps to provide an auxiliary aid or service where that would either—

- enable or facilitate a disabled person's enjoyment of the premises or use of any benefit or facility conferred with the letting; or

- (as the case may be) enable or make it easier for a disabled person to take a letting of the premises.

146. The duty would apply if, were the auxiliary aid or service not provided, it would be impossible or unreasonably difficult for a disabled person or occupier to enjoy the premises, to make use of any benefit or facility they were entitled to use or (as the case may be) to take a letting.

147. For example, a landlord or manager may need to put correspondence in large print for a visually impaired tenant or provide a clip-on receiver (which vibrates when the door bell rings) for a tenant who has a hearing impairment . However the landlord/manager would not have to provide an auxiliary aid or service unless it was needed specifically in connection with the premises concerned. So, he would not, for instance, be obliged to provide a wheelchair for a tenant who had difficulty in walking: the tenant would need this for general purposes, and not just moving around the flat or house let to him by the landlord. (See new sections 24C and 24J(1) and (2)).

148. These duties would <u>not</u> require the making of any alteration to the physical features of premises by a landlord or manager (see new sections 24E(1) and 24J(5)). However they may place a controller of premises, in an appropriate case, under a duty to change or waive a term of the letting which prohibits any alterations to the premises, to the extent necessary to allow a tenant, with the consent of the landlord[6] to make (at his own expense and subject to reasonable conditions including conditions as to reinstatement) alterations needed by reason of the disabled occupier's disability.

149. If the terms of the letting are modified to permit an alteration with the landlord's consent, then the provisions of new section 49G (inserted by section 16) would apply. Section 16 makes procedural and evidential provision as to the withholding of consent to disability-related "improvements" by a landlord, and also provides for the Disability Rights Commission to issue a code of practice and provide conciliation services and support in disputes.

150. The Government intends to make regulations setting out the circumstances in which it is reasonable for a landlord to have to modify or waive a term in a lease prohibiting the making of alterations to a let dwelling house, where that term makes it impossible or unreasonably difficult for a disabled person to enjoy the premises. The exemptions to the duty of reasonable adjustment described below, i.e. the

---

[6] Where a term in the letting permits alterations with the landlord's consent, a requirement that consent is not to be unreasonably withheld would normally be read into that revised term even if not specifically provided for. This is because section 19(2) of the Landlord and Tenant Act 1927 provides that a condition in a lease or tenancy agreement forbidding a tenant from carrying out improvements to the premises without the landlord's consent is to be read as one saying that such consent is not to be unreasonably withheld.

exemptions for small dwellings and the landlord's principal or only home, would operate.

151.   A landlord or manager would not have to take any steps under the new provisions unless requested to do so by the tenant or prospective tenant (see new sections 24C(1), 24D(1) and (2) and 24J(1) and (3)).

152.   The provisions do not apply to premises which are, or have been at any time, the principal or only home of the landlord or manager (see new sections 24B(1) and 24H(1)).

153.   These provisions also do not apply to a landlord or manager who lives on the premises where there is not normally residential accommodation on the premises for more than six persons, or the premises do not contain residential accommodation for more than two other households besides that occupied by the landlord or manager and members of his household. This is the exemption currently provided in section 23 of the DDA (see new sections 24B(3) and (4), and 24H(3) and (4)). However, the exemption can be limited or ended under section 14 of the 2005 Act.

154.   In limited circumstances, a landlord or manager may justify less favourable treatment or a failure to take reasonable steps: see new section 24K. Where he or she can do so, no unlawful discrimination occurs. Section 24K(3) would allow the Secretary of State in regulations to amend, add to or remove the conditions under which a person's failure to comply with a reasonable adjustment duty can be justified.

155.   New section 24F makes special provision where a landlord or manager has incurred costs in taking steps under the new duties in the case of a disabled person lawfully occupying the premises but who is not the tenant (for example, a disabled child of the tenant). This new section makes it unlawful for the landlord/manager to victimise that tenant (whether or not he is disabled) by, for instance, evicting him or increasing the rent.   (Section 22 of the DDA, read with section 55, would make it unlawful for a landlord to evict a disabled tenant because the latter asked for a reasonable adjustment to be made on account of his own disability or to evict any tenant, whether or not disabled, solely because the tenant asked for a reasonable adjustment to be made for the benefit of a disabled person who lawfully occupies the premises but is not a tenant.)

156.   New section 24L(1) confers power on the Secretary of State to make supplementary provisions by regulations, for example to prescribe what steps it is reasonable for a landlord to have to take, or what constitutes an auxiliary aid or physical feature.

157.   New section 24L(2) makes it clear that the regulations made under subsection (1)(a) can provide for a commonhold unit to be treated as let to a person where that person is a unit-holder.

158.   It would be contrary to sections 22 to 24 of the DDA for a landlord/manager to

single out for increase any one tenant's rent or service charge in order to pay for the cost of steps taken under the new provisions inserted by section 13: see the amendments made to section 24 by paragraph 19 of Schedule 1 (and the notes on that provision below). The landlord may make an "across the board" increase to all his tenants (including the disabled tenant) to cover costs.

Section 14: Power to modify or end small dwellings exemption

159. Section 14 confers a power on the Secretary of State to amend, by order, the exemption for small dwellings for the purpose of: adding to the conditions for entitlement to the exemptions provided for in sections 23, 24B and 24H; making any of the conditions for entitlement to those exemptions more onerous; making the conditions for entitlement to those exemptions more onerous overall; otherwise restricting the cases in which any of those exemptions is available; or removing those exemptions.

160. The small dwellings exemption is set out in section 23 and new section 24B(3) and (4) and new section 24H(3) and (4) of the DDA (as inserted by section 13). Broadly speaking, the exemption applies where the landlord or manager shares living accommodation with those not of his own household and either the landlord or manager lets out accommodation in the premises to not more than two other households, or there is not normally residential accommodation on the premises for more than six persons in addition to the landlord or manager and members of his household.

161. Where the exemption applies, the provisions of section 22 and new sections 24A and 24G of the DDA do not apply.

162. Any order to modify or end any of those exemptions relating to small dwellings is subject to the affirmative resolution procedure, i.e. the order must be laid in draft before, and approved by a resolution of, each House of Parliament.

Section 15: General qualifications bodies

163. Section 15 inserts a new Chapter 2A (sections 31AA to 31AF) into Part 4 of the DDA.   These provisions prohibit unlawful discrimination against disabled persons by general qualifications bodies, in relation to the award of relevant qualifications. The prohibitions imposed here reflect, to a large extent, those imposed under sections 14A and 14B of the DDA on qualifications bodies which award trade or professional qualifications. Sections 14A and 14B of the DDA were inserted into Part 2 of that Act by the Amendment Regulations.

164. A "relevant qualification" is one to be prescribed in regulations made by the Secretary of State under new section 31AA(4). It is intended that this power will be used to prescribe qualifications such as A levels, GCSEs and other non-vocational qualifications and their equivalents in Scotland and Wales. But something that is a "trade or professional qualification" within the meaning of section 14A cannot become a relevant qualification (see section 31AA(5)).

165. Under new section 31AA(6)(a) a "general qualifications body" is any

authority or body which can confer a relevant qualification. But this does not include responsible bodies within the meaning of Chapters 1 and 2 of the DDA (e.g. schools), local education authorities in England or Wales, Scottish education authorities, or such authorities or bodies as may be prescribed in regulations to be made by the Secretary of State under subsection (6)(a)(iv).

166.   New sections 31AB and 31AC define what is meant by unlawful discrimination in this context and what is meant by unlawful harassment. The definitions mirror those which apply for the purposes of Part 2 of the DDA in relation to qualifications bodies which confer trade or professional qualifications, by virtue of sections 14A and 14B of the DDA. Therefore, in like manner to sections 14A and 14B of the DDA, if the application of a competence standard by a general qualifications body amounts to less favourable treatment it may only be justified if the standard is applied equally to all persons and its application is a proportionate means of achieving a legitimate aim. A competence standard is any academic, medical or other standard applied by a qualifications body in order to determine whether a person has a particular level of competence or ability.

167.   New section 31AD requires general qualifications bodies in certain circumstances to make reasonable adjustments where disabled persons suffer substantial disadvantage in comparison with others. There is no duty to make reasonable adjustments in relation to competence standards, but the duty is imposed where general qualifications bodies apply provisions, criteria or practices to disabled persons. It also applies in relation to the physical features of premises occupied by general qualifications bodies. This would mean, for example, that a general qualifications body would need to modify arrangements for disabled persons when they sit examinations in premises provided by the body, for example by ensuring there is appropriate ramp access for candidates who use wheelchairs.

168.   New section 31AD(6) enables the Secretary of State to make regulations to further define, clarify and elaborate on the detailed ambit of the duty to make reasonable adjustments, by, for example, specifying what is meant by a provision, criterion, practice or physical feature, or specifying when any of those things is (or is not) to be taken to have a particular effect.

169.   New section 31AE provides powers to make provision with respect to enforcement matters. There is power to set out how a disabled person may enforce a claim of unlawful discrimination under new Chapter 2A. For example, the regulations could specify the enforcement mechanisms (i.e. the court/tribunal), the remedies and procedural matters, such as time limits and admissibility of evidence, which apply. It is intended that much of the detail which is currently contained in Schedule 3 to the DDA would be set down in these regulations with appropriate amendments and modifications.

170.   New section 31AE(2) and (7) provide power to make provision in regulations about the cases where leasehold premises are occupied by qualifications bodies and how the reasonable adjustment duty impacts in this context. The aim is to mirror section 18A of the DDA and much of the detail contained in Schedule 4 to that Act

but with appropriate modifications as required.

171.   New section 31AE(3) mirrors, in large measure, provisions which are to be found elsewhere in the DDA (see for example paragraph 1 of Schedule 3A to the DDA and section 28P of the DDA). The aim is to prevent any contract or agreement from seeking to oust, limit or contravene the substance of Chapter 2A. Section 31AE(4) provides power to make regulations to elaborate, clarify and modify the operation of subsection (3) in this context.

172.   Before making regulations under the new Chapter 2A, the Secretary of State must consult the Scottish Ministers, the National Assembly for Wales and such other persons as appear to him to be appropriate (see new section 31AF).

Section 16: Improvements to let dwelling houses

173.   Section 16 extends only to England and Wales. Subsection (1) inserts a new Part 5B (Improvements to let dwelling houses) into the DDA. New section 49G of the DDA makes new procedural and evidential provision with regard to consent to improvements to let dwelling houses. A 'dwelling house' is a broad term with an established legal meaning as premises (which could be a house, a part of a house, or a flat) which are suitable for all the major activities of life. New section 49G applies to all leases of residential property other than those which concern a protected tenancy, a statutory tenancy or a secure tenancy (to which similar rights already apply by virtue of the Housing Acts 1980 and 1985). It applies where a lease or tenancy agreement provides that a tenant may make improvements to the premises with the landlord's consent. Where the lease prohibits the making of improvements absolutely, the tenant could seek a reasonable adjustment of the terms of the letting under new sections 24A to 24E (inserted by section 13) where those terms have the effect of making it impossible or unreasonably difficult for the disabled person to enjoy the premises.

174.   New section 49G(2) to (6) set out a number of new procedural and evidential rights which apply where—

- a disabled person is tenant or lawful occupier of the premises,

- the dwelling house is their only or principal home,

- the tenant is entitled under the lease to make improvements to the premises with the consent of the landlord,

- the tenant applies to the landlord to make a 'relevant improvement', and

- the lease does not already provide for those rights.

By subsection (7), an improvement is a relevant improvement if, having regard to the disabled person's disability, it is likely to facilitate his enjoyment of the premises he rents (for example, a grab rail or a walk-in shower). 'Improvement' is defined in subsection (9), using similar terms to those used in the Housing Acts 1980 and 1985.

175.   New section 49H of the DDA makes provision for the Disability Rights Commission ("DRC") to make arrangements to provide conciliation services in relation to a dispute of any description concerning the question whether it is reasonable for a landlord to withhold his consent to making of a relevant improvement to a dwelling house. Therefore, conciliation services may be provided where any question arises as to the unreasonable withholding of consent to a relevant improvement, whatever the legal basis for the dispute. For example, it could be an improvement dispute under the express terms of the lease or any dispute arising from the application of the following provisions: section 19(2) of the Landlord and Tenant Act 1927; sections 81 to 85 of the Housing Act 1980; sections 97 to 99 of the Housing Act 1985; or new section 49G of the DDA. Disputes under the new premises provisions (sections 24A to 24L) as inserted by section 13 may be conciliated by virtue of existing section 28 (conciliation of disputes) of the DDA.

176.   Section 16(2) amends section 53A of the DDA to enable the DRC to issue codes of practice giving practical guidance to landlords and tenants with regard to consent to the making of relevant adjustments (including the application of the other legislation listed in new section 53A(1E) concerning tenants' improvements) and circumstances in which a landlord's refusal of consent to an improvement is unreasonable.

177.   Section 53A is also further amended by paragraph 28 of Schedule 1 so that a court must take account of any provision of the code of practice which appears relevant in any proceedings relating to a relevant improvement, for example in proceedings under section 53 of the Landlord and Tenant Act 1954 which gives a county court, concurrently with the High Court, jurisdiction to make a declaration as to whether a landlord has unreasonably withheld consent to the making of an improvement (even where the tenant seeks no other relief in the proceedings). See also section 86 of the Housing Act 1980 and section 110 of the Housing Act 1985 concerning a county court's power to make a declaration in cases about improvements to premises let under a protected, statutory or secure tenancy.

178.   Section 16(3) amends section 7 of the Disability Rights Commission Act 1999 (provision of assistance in relation to proceedings) to enable the DRC to provide assistance to a tenant or lawful occupier in any proceedings relating to the making of a relevant improvement to a let dwelling house.

Section 17: Generalisation of section 56 of the 1995 Act in relation to Part 3 claims

179.   Section 17 replaces existing section 56 of the DDA. That section currently sets out a framework for a questions and reply procedure which may be used by complainants, prospective or otherwise, in deciding whether to bring a claim or in bringing claims under Part 2 of the DDA. The new section extends that framework so that it will also apply to claims brought or to be brought under Part 3 of the DDA

as amended. The current prescribed forms (both the questionnaire and reply) are set out in S.I. 2004/1168.

Section 18: Meaning of "disability"

180. Section 1 of the DDA defines a person as having a disability for the purposes of the DDA where he has a physical or mental impairment which has a substantial and long-term adverse effect on his ability to carry out normal day-to-day activities. This definition is supplemented by Schedule 1 to the DDA, which elaborates on, and sets out other, circumstances in which a person is to be treated as disabled and therefore as meeting the definition in section 1. In particular, in Schedule 1 to the DDA: paragraph 1(1) deals with mental impairments; paragraph 7(5) deals with persons deemed to be disabled; and paragraph 8 provides that a person with a progressive condition such as HIV infection, multiple sclerosis (MS) or cancer is to be treated as disabled where the impairment has an effect on his ability to carry out normal day-to-day activities, even where it is less than substantial, provided that the effects are likely to become substantial in the future. All three of these supplementary provisions are affected by section 18.

181. Section 18(2) removes the requirement in paragraph 1(1) of Schedule 1 to the DDA that a mental illness must be "clinically well-recognised" before it can amount to a mental impairment for the purposes of section 1. The removal of this requirement does not affect the need for people with a mental illness to demonstrate that they have an impairment which has a long-term and substantial adverse effect on their ability to carry out normal day-to-day activities.

182. Section 18(3) inserts a new paragraph 6A into Schedule 1 to the DDA. New paragraph 6A(1) deems people with HIV, cancer or MS to be disabled before they experience any of the effects described in section 1 of, or paragraph 8 of Schedule 1 to, the DDA. New paragraph 6A(2) and (3) enable the Secretary of State to make regulations excluding persons who have cancer of a prescribed description from the provisions of sub-paragraph (1). This power could be exercised, for example, to exclude those types of cancer which do not require substantial treatment. Any regulations made under this power are subject to the affirmative resolution procedure: see the new section 67(4)(h) inserted by paragraph 33(5) of Schedule 1.

183. Paragraph 7(5) of Schedule 1 to the DDA contains a power to deem a person to have a disability in prescribed circumstances and hence to be a disabled person for the purposes of the DDA[7]. New paragraph 7(5A) is inserted into Schedule 1 to the DDA by section 18(4) in order to make it clear that there are no implied limitations on the power in paragraph 7(5) of that Schedule. Regulations made under paragraph 7(5) will then be able to deem any group of people to be disabled, even a group covered in some way by another provision of Schedule 1 to the DDA (such as persons with a progressive condition (other than MS, HIV infection or cancer) or persons who will, for some other reason, not be protected by either section 1 of, or Schedule 1 to, the DDA).

---

[7] Regulations have been made under this power: see the Disability Discrimination (Blind and Partially Sighted Persons) Regulations 2003 (S.I. 2003/712).

184. Section 18(5) inserts a new paragraph 9 into Schedule 1 to the DDA to define HIV infection in recognition of the fact that there are two strains of the Human Immunodeficiency Virus recognised as capable of causing AIDS in human beings.

Section 20: Short title, interpretation, commencement and extent

185. By subsection (7), the 2005 Act generally does not extend to Northern Ireland. This is despite the fact that the DDA, as originally enacted, extends to Northern Ireland as well – but with the modifications referred to in Schedule 8 to the DDA. The reason for this discrepancy, as explained in the note on territorial extent above, is that discrimination is now a transferred matter under the Northern Ireland Act 1998.

186. The blue badge provisions (as defined in subsection (9)) and section 16 (improvements to let dwelling houses) do not extend to Scotland: see subsections (8) and (9). The regulation of parking permits for disabled persons falls within the legislative competence of the Scottish Parliament. The Scottish Executive is considering what steps to take regarding the making of disability-related improvements.

SCHEDULE 1

Minor and Consequential Amendments
Part 1

Amendments to the DDA 1995
Paragraph 2
187. The amendments made by sub-paragraphs (2) and (4) ensure that the provisions of the DDA relating to past disabilities (section 2 and Schedule 2) apply to the duties under sections 49A and 49D (inserted by section 3). See also the amendment to Schedule 2 made by paragraph 37.

Paragraph 3
188. Paragraph 3(2) inserts a new subsection (A1) into section 3 of the DDA. Section 3 of the DDA, as currently drafted, enables the Secretary of State to issue guidance on two aspects of the definition of disability: whether an impairment is to be considered as having a substantial adverse effect on a person's ability to carry out normal day-to-day activities; and whether an impairment is to be considered as having a long-term effect. New section 3(A1) enables the Secretary of State to issue guidance on all aspects of the definition of disability. For the purposes of new paragraph 6A of Schedule 1, this would enable guidance to be issued, for example, on when a person is to be considered as having HIV infection, cancer or MS or on what constitutes substantial treatment.

Paragraph 5

189.   This makes changes to section 4C(2) in order to ensure that new section 21B(8) and (9) do not cause new section 21B(1) to apply in relation to an office or post mentioned in new section 15B(3)(b) inserted by section 1. By reason of the effect of section 4F(1), the amendment does not affect the operation of sections 4D and 4E.

Paragraph 6

190.   This replaces subsection (3) of section 14C DDA (practical work experience, which was inserted by regulation 13 of the Amendment Regulations). The new subsection restates with modifications the matters to which sections 14C and 14D do not apply.

Paragraph 7

191.   This makes changes to section 16A(2) (meaning of "relevant relationship" in section 16A). Sub-paragraph (a) ensures that the relationships between locally-electable authorities and their members are not covered by section 16A (relationships which have come to an end) because that section, which was inserted by the Amendment Regulations, relates to the provisions in Part 2 of the DDA governing the employment field and has no application to the relationships governed by new sections 15A to 15C (councillors and members of the Greater London Authority).

192.   Sub-paragraph (b) makes changes to section 16A(2)(b) in consequence of the new definition of "employment services", applying to the whole of the DDA, to be inserted by paragraph 34(2) into section 68(1) of the DDA.

Paragraph 8

193.   Sub-paragraph (2) inserts a new subsection (2C) into section 16B (discriminatory advertisements) of the DDA and ensures that section 16B(1) will not apply to advertisements inviting applications from persons in their capacity as members of a locally-electable authority for a relevant appointment or benefit which the authority is intending to make or confer. This is because section 16B, which was inserted into the DDA by the Amendment Regulations, relates to the provisions in Part 2 of the DDA governing the employment field and has no application to the relationships governed by new sections 15A to 15C (councillors and members of the Greater London Authority).

Paragraph 10

194.   This amends section 17B (enforcement of section 16B and 16C), and is necessary in consequence of the creation of the new criminal offence in section 16B(2B) (discriminatory advertisements), inserted by section 10(3). Without the amendment the Disability Rights Commission would be the prosecuting authority for such offences, and proceedings would have to be presented to an employment tribunal. Paragraph 38(2) provides for a related amendment to Schedule 3 of the DDA to allow for the bringing of criminal proceedings for offences under section 16B(2B).

Paragraph 11

195.	This makes two consequential amendments to section 18D(2). Sub-paragraph (a) ensures that any reference to the "duty to make reasonable adjustments" in Part 2 of the DDA includes a reference to the duty imposed on locally-electable authorities under section 15C. Sub-paragraph (b) ensures that the definition of "physical feature" in section 18D(2) (as inserted by the Amendment Regulations) is without prejudice to the power in new section 15C(4)(e) to make provision as to things which are, and things which are not, to be treated as physical features for the purposes of the duty on locally-electable authorities to make reasonable adjustments.

Paragraph 12

196.	This inserts new section 18E into the DDA (premises provided otherwise than in course of a Part 2 relationship). The new section is intended to clarify the boundaries between Part 2 of the DDA (the employment field and members of locally-electable authorities) and Part 3 (discrimination in other areas) with respect to the provision of premises for persons such as employees. The general effect is that, where accommodation is provided in the course of a person's employment (for example live-in accommodation), any related discrimination or harassment will be governed by Part 2 of the DDA. But where the accommodation is provided on a separate basis, unconnected with a person's employment (for example, where a council employee is a tenant of the same local authority) then section 18E will ensure that Part 2 does not apply. New section 18E needs to be read with new section 24M (premises provisions not to operate where other provisions apply), discussed below.

Paragraph 13

197.	Sub-paragraphs (2) and (3) make minor and consequential amendments to section 19 (goods, facilities and services) in consequence of the new section 21ZA (transport vehicles) inserted by section 5. Sub-paragraph (4) restates and modifies subsection (5A), which makes provision about the relationship between section 19 and Part 4 (education).

Paragraph 14

198.	This replaces section 20(7)(c) in consequence of a non-textual amendment made by paragraph 1 of Schedule 5 to the Adults with Incapacity (Scotland) Act 2000. Section 20(7)(c) allows the Secretary of State to make regulations disapplying section 20(4)(b), which concerns justification by a service provider of less favourable treatment of a disabled person who is incapable of entering into an enforceable agreement. The power will be available where, under the law of Scotland, a guardian, tutor or judicial factor has been appointed to manage the disabled person's affairs.

Paragraph 15

199.	This amends section 21A (inserted in the DDA by the Amendment Regulations with effect from 1 October 2004) in consequence of the new definition of "employment services" inserted in section 68(1) by paragraph 34(2) of Schedule 1, which will apply to the whole of the DDA. It also makes a change to section

21A(4) in consequence of new section 21ZA (transport vehicles) inserted by section 5.

Paragraph 16

200.   This inserts a new subsection (3A) into section 22 of the DDA. Section 22(3) of the DDA forbids discrimination by a person who manages premises against a disabled person occupying those premises. The new subsection confers a power on the Secretary of State to make provision by regulations for the purposes of section 22(3) as to who is, and who is not, to be treated as being (i) a person who manages premises, or (ii) a person occupying premises.

Paragraph 17

201.   This inserts a new section 22A into the DDA. This makes it unlawful for a person (in particular a commonhold association) to discriminate by withholding a licence or consent for the disposal of an interest in a commonhold unit in favour of, or to, a disabled person or by deliberately not being a party to such a disposal. Subsections (1) and (2) contain provisions comparable to those that apply to leasehold premises by virtue of section 22(4). Subsection (3) allows the Secretary of State to make regulations providing for subsections (1) and (2) not to apply, or to apply only, in particular cases.

Paragraph 18

202.   This paragraph amends section 23 (but see also the power conferred by section 14 to restrict or repeal section 23). Section 23 provides for an exemption from section 22 of the DDA (discrimination in relation to premises) for small dwellings. The exemption applies where a landlord or manager (referred to as the "relevant occupier") lives on premises which, in addition to accommodation for himself and members of his household, either consist of residential accommodation for not more than six persons or consist of residential accommodation for not more than two other households. Subsection (6) of section 23 defines who the "relevant occupier" is for the purposes of that section. However that subsection omits to spell out who is the "relevant occupier" for the purposes of applying the small dwellings exemption to section 22(3) (discrimination by a manager of premises).   The amendment will provide that the "relevant occupier" for the purposes of applying the exemption to section 22(3) is the person managing the premises or a near relative of his.

Paragraph 19

203.   Sub-paragraph (2) inserts in section 24 of the DDA a reference to new section 22A (which is itself inserted into the DDA by paragraph 17 of Schedule 1). This ensures that the provisions of section 24 on discrimination and justification apply also to new section 22A.

204.   Sub-paragraphs (3) and (4) further amend section 24 of the DDA by inserting new paragraphs (e) and (f) into subsection (3), and new subsections (3A) to (3C). These provide additional circumstances in which treatment which would otherwise be contrary to section 22(1) or (3) can be justified, i.e. where a person letting or proposing to let premises to a disabled person, or managing rented premises

occupied by a disabled person, incurs additional costs as a result of the disabled person's disability. But the landlord/manager may not justify charging such additional costs where these are incurred in taking any steps required under new section 24C, 24D or 24J (reasonable adjustments) inserted by section 13. This is broadly consistent with the position which applies under sections 19 to 21 (service providers): see in particular, section 20(4)(e) and (5).

205.   Sub-paragraph (5) makes one other minor amendment to section 24 of the DDA by inserting a new subsection (4A). This would allow the Secretary of State to provide by regulations for subsection (3)(b) not to apply in prescribed circumstances. Section 24(3)(b) allows a person disposing of premises, or a manager of premises, to justify less favourable treatment of a disabled person who is incapable of entering into an enforceable agreement. The amendment would bring section 24 into line with section 20, which also contains a power (see subsection (7)) enabling the Secretary of State to disapply the corresponding justification in section 20(4)(b) in certain circumstances.

Paragraph 20

206.   This inserts new section 24M of the DDA (premises provisions do not apply where other provisions operate). The new section is designed to deal with potential overlaps between the premises provisions contained in sections 22 to 24 and new sections 24A to 24L (inserted by section 13), and other relevant provisions of the DDA. The general intention is that the premises provisions should not apply to cases where other provisions do so. In particular, new section 24M excludes premises provided to a student or pupil in the Part 4 field (education) (section 24M(1)(c)), and premises provided in the course of a "Part 2 relationship" (such as an employment relationship)(section 24M(1)(b), see also new section 18E). It also excludes from the ambit of sections 22 to 24L cases where a provider of services provides the premises in providing services to the public (for example, the provision of holiday accommodation by a tour operator)(section 24M(1)(a)). The intention is that sections 19 to 21, and not the premises provisions, should apply to such a case. There is a power in section 24M(2) which will allow the Secretary of State to prescribe exemptions from section 24(1)(a) if the need for more precise demarcation arises. The premises provisions also do not apply where the provisions relating to private clubs do so (section 24M(1)(d)).

Paragraph 21

207.   This paragraph replaces subsections (7) and (8) of section 25 of the DDA (which were inserted by the Amendment Regulations, regulation 19(2)). The new provisions (which should be read with section 11 of the 2005 Act and section 21A of the DDA) ensure that employment tribunals have jurisdiction to consider complaints arising from discrimination by insurers in the provision of group insurance services contrary to section 19 of the DDA, and discrimination or harassment in the provision of "employment services" contrary to section 19 or section 21A(2). See also the notes above on section 11.

Paragraph 22

208. This substitutes subsection (1A)[8] of section 26 (which renders void certain terms of agreements, for example those which require the commission of unlawful acts of discrimination). The new provision ensures that section 26 does not apply to terms of contracts or other agreements relating to employment services or group insurance arrangements. (Such terms are to be covered by Schedule 3A to the DDA instead: see paragraph 39 below)

Paragraph 23

209. This makes minor and consequential amendments to section 27 (alterations to premises occupied under leases) resulting from the duties imposed on public authorities under new sections 21B to 21E (see commentary on section 2) and on associations under new sections 21F and 21J (see commentary on section 12).

Paragraph 24

210. This paragraph makes a minor amendment to the regulation-making powers in section 28D in Part 4 of the DDA (under which local authorities are required to prepare plans and strategies to make schools accessible for disabled pupils) in order to make clear the meaning of "regulations" for the purposes of that section, and to ensure consistency with the revised definitions of "prescribed" and "regulations" in section 68(1) (as inserted by paragraph 34(5) and (6) below).

Paragraph 25

211. This amends section 31B (conciliation of disputes under Part 4) in consequence of the insertion by section 15 of the 2005 Act of the new Chapter 2A into Part 4 (which concerns general qualifications bodies).

Paragraph 26

212. This amends section 33 (hire car services at designated transport facilities). It provides that functions of the Secretary of State to make regulations under this section, so far as exercisable in relation to transport facilities in Scotland, are exercisable by the Scottish Ministers. It replaces the equivalent provision made by the Scotland Act 1998 (Transfer of Functions to the Scottish Ministers etc.) Order 1999 (S.I. 1999/1750), in which the entry relating to section 33 of the DDA is revoked. The amendment preserves the Secretary of State's existing power to legislate in respect of Scotland under section 2(2) of the European Communities Act 1972. The amendments are being made in the interest of transparency and greater clarity given that, for technical reasons, it is necessary to refer expressly to regulations and orders made under section 33 in amendments to sections 67 and 68 made by the 2005 Act.

Paragraph 27

213. Sub-paragraph (a) removes section 46(3) and (4) of the DDA, which made it a criminal offence to use a regulated rail vehicle for carriage which did not comply with rail vehicle accessibility regulations ("RVAR"). Section 46(3) and (4) are

---

[8] Section 26(1A) is inserted into the DDA by the Amendment Regulations with effect from 1st October 2004.

replaced by new sections 47D to 47L (inserted by section 8 of the 2005 Act) which introduce a civil enforcement regime.

214.   Sub-paragraph (b) amends the definition of "regulated rail vehicle" in section 46(6) of the DDA to ensure that a vehicle is regulated even when some and not all of the provisions of RVAR apply. This might occur if the Secretary of State were to prescribe that vehicles which are refurbished must comply with certain requirements of the RVAR.

Paragraph 28
215.   This makes amendments to section 53A so as to allow the Disability Rights Commission to issue codes of practice in relation to: discrimination by public authorities, associations and general qualifications bodies (see sections 2, 12 and 15); and the exercise by public authorities of the duties to be imposed by or under new sections 49A and 49D (inserted by section 3). (Note that section 16(2) amends section 53A to provide for the issues of codes of pratice in relation to a landlord's consent to the making of improvements by a tenant.) This paragraph also amends section 53A so as to provide for the taking into account of the provisions of a code of practice in relevant proceedings, including proceedings relating to a disability-related improvement to a dwelling house occupied by a disabled person (as to which, see section 16).

Paragraph 29
216.   Sub-paragraph (2) amends section 55(1) (victimisation) so as to disapply it from new sections 24A to 24L (which require landlords and managers to provide reasonable adjustments in certain circumstances for disabled people). This is because victimisation of a disabled person in relation to the letting of premises is already provided for by the interaction of sections 22 to 24 with section 55, and by the provisions of new section 24F.

217.   Sub-paragraph (3) amends section 55(2)(a)(iii) of the DDA by inserting after "done anything under" the words "or by reference to". This applies and generalises in relation to Parts 2 to 4 of the DDA the provisions of subsection (6) (inserted by the Amendment Regulations) which apply only for the purposes of Part 2. Subsection (6) is consequently repealed.

218.   Sub-paragraph (4) ensures that section 55 applies to a non-disabled person who is discriminated against under section 15B (councillors, and members of the GLA) (inserted by section 1).

Paragraph 30
219.   This amends section 59(1) (statutory authority). Section 59(1) provides that nothing in the DDA makes unlawful any act done in pursuance of any enactment, or in pursuance of any instrument made by a Minister of the Crown under any enactment, or to comply with any condition or requirement imposed by a Minister of the Crown by virtue of any enactment. The amendment applies section 59(1) to acts done in pursuance of instruments made by, and conditions or requirements imposed by, a member of the Scottish Executive, or the National Assembly for

Wales.

Paragraph 31

220.   This inserts a new subsection (A1) into section 64 of the DDA so that the new sections 21B to 21E (inserted by section 2) and new Part 5A (inserted by section 3), which concern acts of public authorities, apply to the Crown. Provision is also made for Crown liability in respect of acts of Crown servants within the scope of new sections 21B to 21E and new Part 5A.

Paragraph 32

221.   This is a minor consequential amendment to section 65 (application to Parliament). Subsection (5), which relates to proceedings before employment tribunals under Part 2 of the DDA, is amended in consequence of the fact that certain claims under Part 3 (in respect of employment services and group insurance) will also be dealt with before employment tribunals.

Paragraph 33

222.   This makes various amendments to section 67 of the DDA. Sub-paragraphs (2) and (3) tidy up section 67(1) and (3)(a), in particular to make provision for cases where the DDA confers regulation-making powers on devolved authorities (see sections 28D, 33 and 49D(3) and (4)).

223.   Sub-paragraph (4) inserts new subsections (3A), (3B) and (3C) into section 67 of the DDA. Subsection (3A) provides that if regulations are made under new section 21D(7)(b) which omit new section 21D(5), there is power to make necessary consequential amendments to new section 21D. Subsection (3C) ensures that regulations made under section 49D imposing specific duties on public authorities can amend or repeal provisions in Acts of Parliament, Acts of the Scottish Parliament or subordinate legislation where this is necessary to make the specific duties effective, for example, because of a conflict with an existing duty or obligation.

224.   Sub-paragraph (5) substitutes new subsections (4), (4A) to (4D), (5) and (5A) for the existing subsections (4) and (5) of section 67.

225.   New subsections (4) and (4A) provide for the use of the affirmative Parliamentary procedure in the following cases:

-   the first regulations made under new section 21H(1) (imposition of duty to make adjustments in relation to associations);

-   the first regulations to be made under sections 31AE(1), (2) and (4) (general qualifications bodies) and any regulations made under those provisions which amend the DDA;

-   regulations under section 31AE(1) that make provision as to remedies;

- regulations made under section 47J(3) (determining the turnover of a rail vehicle operator for the purpose of imposing a penalty);

- regulations made under 49D(1) or (2) that make consequential amendments to an Act of Parliament or an Act of the Scottish Parliament;

- regulations made under section 67A(3) (setting out the basis on which the Secretary of State will exercise his discretion as to which of the parliamentary procedures available to him under section 67(5A) (the draft affirmative procedure or the negative resolution procedure) should be used when making an order under section 47(1) (exemptions from rail vehicle accessibility regulations));

- regulations made under paragraph 6A(2) of Schedule 1 (excluding certain types of cancers from the extended definition of disability in paragraph 6A(1)).

226. New subsections (4B) and (4C) provide for regulations made by the Scottish Ministers under new section 49D, which make consequential amendments to either an Act of Parliament or an Act of the Scottish Parliament, to be made under the affirmative procedure in the Scottish Parliament.

227. New subsection (4D) provides for other types of regulations made by the Scottish Ministers under section 49D or regulations or orders made by them under section 33 to be subject to negative procedure in the Scottish Parliament.

228. New subsection (5) provides for the negative procedure (at the Westminster Parliament) to apply to all other regulations made under the DDA by the Secretary of State, and all orders made by the Secretary of State except for: appointed day orders made under any of sections 3(9), 53A(6)(a) and 70(3); and exemption orders made under section 47(1).

229. New subsection (5A) provides that orders made under section 47(1) (exemption from rail vehicle accessibility regulations) can be made by either the draft affirmative or the negative resolution procedure. The Secretary of State, in determining which of the parliamentary procedures should be used, must exercise his discretion subject to new section 67A which, in particular, enables him to make regulations setting out the basis on which he will make that decision. Until such regulations are in place, all orders made under section 47(1) will be subject to the draft affirmative resolution procedure.

Paragraph 34

230. This inserts a number of definitions into section 68(1). These include the terms "criminal investigation", "criminal proceedings" and public investigator functions" for the purposes of new sections 21C and 56, and (by cross-reference to section 21A) the term "employment services" which will apply for the purposes of the DDA as a whole. Some other   definitions are slightly amended.

Paragraph 36

231.   This replaces the reference to "infection by the human immunodeficiency virus" in paragraph 8 of Schedule 1 to the DDA with a reference to "HIV infection" in recognition of the fact that there is more than one strain of HIV recognised as capable of causing AIDS in human beings.

Paragraph 38

232.   This makes amendments to Schedule 3 to the DDA (enforcement and procedure). Sub-paragraph (2) ensures that criminal proceedings may be brought in respect of the new offence in new section 16B(2B) (discriminatory advertisements) inserted by section 10. Sub-paragraph (8) makes a similar amendment in respect of the offence under section 28J(9).

233.   The amendments made by sub-paragraphs (3), (4), (6), (7) and (9) to (13) tie in with the amendments (made by paragraph 30) to section 59(1)(b) and (c) of the DDA and are made in view of the 1998 devolution settlements with Scotland and Wales. Amendments are made to paragraphs 4, 8, 9, 11 and 15 of Schedule 3 to the DDA to provide for the Scottish Ministers or the National Assembly for Wales to be able to certify that they have imposed a condition or requirement and that it was in operation at a specified time. The certificate is to be treated by the court or tribunal as conclusive evidence of the matters specified in proceedings brought under sections 17A, 25, 25(8), 28I, 28K, 28L, 28N and 28V of the DDA.

234.   Amendments are made by sub-paragraph (5) in consequence of the insertion in Part 3 of the DDA of new section 21B (discrimination by public authorities) (see section 2). The amendments allow for the staying or (in Scotland) sisting of proceedings brought under section 25 of the DDA which might affect a criminal investigation or criminal proceedings. They also provide for the restriction of remedies under a section 21B claim which relates to criminal matters.

Paragraph 39

235.   Sub-paragraph (2) inserts a new paragraph 2(3)(d) into Schedule 3A[9] (validity of contracts) enabling the Secretary of State to prescribe an additional description of persons to be treated as a "relevant independent adviser" for the purposes of making a compromise contract to settle a complaint to which sections 17A(1) or 25(8) apply (that is, complaints about employment or related matters, group insurance and employment services). This reinstates without change a power which existed in the DDA prior to 1 October 2004 that for technical reasons could not be included in the Amendment Regulations.

236.   Sub-paragraph (3) replaces paragraph 11 of Schedule 3A with new paragraphs 11 and 12. The new provisions ensure that Schedule 3A (which renders void certain terms of contracts, for example those which require the commission of unlawful acts of discrimination) will cover terms of contracts or other agreements relating to employment services or group insurance.

---

[9] Schedule 3A was inserted into the DDA by the Amendment Regulations with effect from 1st October 2004.

Paragraph 40

237. Sub-paragraphs (2), (5) and (6) amend Schedule 4 (failure to obtain consent to an alteration to leased premises) so as to ensure that employment tribunals hear cases under section 25(8) to which section 27 applies (claims of discrimination involving alterations to leased premises occupied by a provider of employment services or group insurance). In particular, new paragraph 7A inserted into Schedule 4 by sub-paragraph (6) enables the tribunal to cause lessors to be joined as parties in certain circumstances.

238. Sub-paragraphs (3) and (4) extend the application of the provisions of Schedule 4 to premises leased by public authorities and associations (see sections 2 and 12 respectively).

PART 2

Amendments related to disabled persons' badges

Paragraph 41

239. This amends section 21(4) of the Chronically Sick and Disabled Persons Act 1970 ("CSDPA 1970") which currently refers to bodies which care for disabled people, and to which "blue badges" can be issued, as "institutions". This is considered to be an out-dated and rather offensive term, so it is replaced by a reference to "organisation".

Paragraphs 42 to 44

240. These changes follow from the recognition of non-GB disabled persons' badges – "recognised badges" – under section 9 of the 2005 Act. The Road Traffic Regulation Act 1984 ("RTRA 1984") provides that vehicles displaying British blue badges should not be immobilised (section 105 of RTRA 1984), but that wrongful use of a blue badge or any consequential avoidance of clamping constitutes an offence (sections 105(5) and 117 of RTRA 1984 respectively). These paragraphs insert into RTRA 1984 corresponding provisions in respect of recognised badges.

Paragraph 45

241. This paragraph makes amendments that determine the penalties for the new offences relating to the wrongful use of recognised badges discussed above.

Paragraphs 46 to 48

242. These paragraphs are consequential to the new sections inserted into CSDPA 1970 by section 9. The amendments to the Road Traffic Act 1991 and to the Traffic Management Act 2004 are analogous to the amendments to the Road Traffic Regulation Act 1984 discussed above. They provide exemptions from clamping in favour of vehicles displaying recognised badges, and for offences relating to the misuse of a recognised badge.

PART 3

Other Amendments

Paragraph 49

243.   This inserts a new subsection (3A) into section 18 of the Disabled Persons (Services, Consultation and Representation) Act 1986 to ensure that when regulations are made by the National Assembly for Wales under that Act they are not subject to the scrutiny of the Westminster Parliament in pursuance of subsection (3) of that section.

Paragraph 50

244.   This paragraph makes various amendments to the Disability Rights Commission Act 1999 in consequence of the amendments to the DDA made by section 15 (general qualification bodies) and section 16 (improvements to let dwelling houses). It also provides for the repeal of section 11 of that Act, which amended a provision that has since been repealed.

SCHEDULE 2

245.   Schedule 2 provides for the repeal of certain provisions in the DDA and in other enactments in consequence of amendments made by the 2005 Act.

COMMENCEMENT

246.   Section 20 provides for the 2005 Act's provisions, with the exception of section 20 itself and the blue badge provisions, to come into force on such day or days as the Secretary of State may by order appoint. Section 20 itself will come into force on Royal Assent. The blue badge provisions (i.e. section 9 and the related consequential amendments and repeals) will be brought into force in England by order made by the Secretary of State and in Wales by order made by the National Assembly for Wales.

HANSARD REFERENCES

Stage	Date	Hansard Reference
House of Lords		
Introduction	25 November 2004	Vol. 667 Col 161
Second Reading	6 December 2005	Vol. 667 Cols. 665 - 711
Grand Committee	13 January 2005	Vol. 668 Cols. GC57 – GC122
	17 January 2005	Vol. 668 Cols. GC123 – GC190
	20 January 2005	Vol. 668 Cols. GC307 – GC364
Report	3 February 2005	Vol. 669 Cols. 363 – 450
	8 February 2005	Vol. 669 Cols. 665 - 692
Third Reading	28 February 2005	Vol. 670 Cols. 48 – 87
House of Commons		
Introduction	1 March 2005	N/A
Second Reading	23 March 2005	Vol. 432 Cols. 898 - 966
Committee and Third Reading	6 April 2005	Vol. 432 Cols. 1500 - 1511
House of Lords		
Consideration of Commons amendments	7 April 2005	Vol. 671 Cols. 911 - 918

Royal Assent – 7 April 2005   House of Lords Hansard Vol. 671 Col. 950

House of Commons Hansard Vol. 432 Col. 1641

Printed in the UK by The Stationery Office Limited
under the authority and superintendence of Carol Tullo, Controller of
Her Majesty's Stationery Office and Queen's Printer of Acts of Parliament.

4/2005   305998   19585